The Wrath of God

The Wrath of God

by
John MacArthur, Jr.

WORD OF GRACE COMMUNICATIONS
P.O. Box 4000
Panorama City, CA 91412

© 1982 by
JOHN MACARTHUR, JR.

Moody Press Edition, 1986

ISBN: 0-8024-5096-2

1 2 3 4 5 6 7 Printing/GB/Year 91 90 89 88 87 86

Printed in the United States of America

Contents

These Bible studies are taken from messages delivered by Pastor-Teacher John MacArthur, Jr., at Grace Community Church in Panorama City, California. These messages have been combined into a 6-tape album entitled *The Wrath of God*. You may purchase this series either in an attractive vinyl cassette album or as individual cassettes. To purchase these tapes, request the album *The Wrath of God* or ask for the tapes by their individual GC numbers. Please consult the current price list; then, send your order, making your check payable to:

WORD OF GRACE COMMUNICATIONS
P.O. Box 4000
Panorama City, CA 91412

Or, call the following toll-free number:
1-800-55-GRACE

1

The Gospel of Christ

Outline

A. The Heart of the Apostle
   1. His example
   2. Our escape
   3. The exhortation
B. The Heart of the Epistle

Lesson

I. Power
   A. The Dichotomy
      1. Man's desire
      2. Man's deficiency
         a) His inability to change what he is
         b) His misunderstanding of what can change him
      3. God's deliverance
   B. The Dilemma
      1. 1 Corinthians 1:18
      2. 1 Corinthians 1:23-24
      3. 1 Corinthians 2:1-5
   C. The Description
      1. In the Old Testament
      2. In the New Testament
II. Salvation
   A. Its Definition
   B. Its Dimension
      1. Present
         a) Salvation from life's infection
         b) Salvation from lostness
      2. Future
         a) Salvation from death and hell
         b) Salvation from inevitable judgment by God's wrath

C. Its Desire
D. Its Divine Necessity
   1. Man's condition
   2. God's provision
III. Faith
  A. The Predicate of Faith
  B. The Object of Faith
    1. Replaced
    2. Recognized
  C. The Subjects of Faith
IV. Righteousness
  A. Activated
  B. Imparted

Introduction

Romans 1:16-17 contains the most life-transforming truths ever put into men's hands. If we really understand and respond to the truths in these two verses, time and eternity will be totally altered. I believe that they form the theme and thesis for the entire epistle to the Romans. In brief but glorious and comprehensive terms, the epistle is compressed into these basic truths. These verses are a statement of the gospel of Christ. In the beginning of chapter 1 Paul briefly discusses the message and himself as its messenger; then he goes on to crystalize the thesis of the epistle, the gospel of Christ, and reveal his boldness in declaring it.

A. The Heart of the Apostle

1. His example

Paul said, "For I am not ashamed of the gospel of Christ" (v. 16a). All the learned religionists and all the philosophers of Rome did not intimidate Paul; nor did they intimidate him in:

a) Galatia—Acts 14:5-6, 19-21

b) Philippi—Acts 16:19-25

c) Thessalonica—Acts 17:5-10a

d) Berea—Acts 17:13-14

e) Athens—Acts 17:18, 32

f) Corinth—Acts 18:6, 12-18a

g) Ephesus—Acts 19:23-30

2

h) Jerusalem—Acts 21:27-36; 22:22-24

Paul endured every kind of verbal and physical persecution at the hands of the opponents of the gospel, yet he calmly viewed the disdain of the unbelievers, understanding the contempt and ridicule of those who rejected Christ. He faced death itself for the gospel, but never once did he become ashamed of Christ. He would face anybody, anytime, and preach Jesus Christ.

2. Our escape

All of us would like to be able to identify with Paul. But the fact is, very often you and I are ashamed of the gospel of Christ. In those times when we could speak, we don't. When we could be bold, we aren't. We face the hostility of the world and the unimpressiveness of a gospel that talks about sin and blood and death and sounds so foolish to men. We're afraid of what they might think, so we tend to be silent when we should speak. The same fear of opposition and contempt from the world, which Paul was able to overcome in the power of God, often leads us to be silent or to corrupt and accommodate the message to men.

"Health and Wealth"—Accommodating the Message

There is a new movement in America called the "Health and Wealth" ministries. They're promising people that in Christ one gets physical comfort and possessions. Some people are saying, "Jesus will give you healing. You'll never be sick. Jesus wants you wealthy. Life will be blissful in the physical dimension." They are offering the very thing that Jesus rejected in Matthew 8:19-22.

1. Health—A scribe came to Jesus and said, "Teacher, I will follow You wherever You go." And Jesus said to him, "The foxes have holes, and the birds of the air have nests; but the Son of man has nowhere to lay His head' " (vv. 19-20, NASB*). He said, "Fella, I do not accept you because you're looking for comfort and ease—and I'm not offering that." He wanted comfort, but Jesus said no and rejected him.

2. Wealth—Another of his disciples said unto him, "Lord, permit me first to go and bury my father." But Jesus said unto him, "Follow me, and let the dead bury their dead"

New American Standard Bible.

3

(vv. 21-22). The point was, the man's father wasn't even dead yet—he just wanted to hang around to get the inheritance. He wanted to get his money first, but Jesus turned him down.

3. The exhortation

Two things that keep men from Christ are personal comfort and possessions. When false teachers come and offer to men the very things that keep them from Christ, they thus bypass the real gospel for a phony. We must confront people with the gospel—being so unashamed of its truth that we do not compromise it to accommodate the sin of man.

B. The Heart of the Epistle

Why is Paul so bold? Verse 16 is the key: "For I am not ashamed of the gospel of Christ; for it is the *power of God* unto salvation"(italics added). He is bold to preach the gospel because of what it is and what it does. The reason Paul was not overcome by the temptation to be ashamed of the gospel, but rather proclaimed it so joyously, was that it is powerful and it changes lives. Sure it's a stumbling block, and of course it's foolishness (1 Cor. 1:23), but it's also "the power of God unto salvation to everyone that believeth," and he knew that. Paul's supreme passion was to see men saved. He even said in Romans 9:3 that he could wish himself accursed for the sake of seeing the salvation of his people. He didn't care about his personal comfort, his reputation, or his popularity. His life offered no compromise to a clear, confrontive gospel. He preached the gospel because he knew it was the power of God that could change people.

Understanding the gospel of Christ comes to us in understanding four key words in this passage—"power," "salvation," "believeth," and "righteousness." If you understand their meaning, you understand the gospel.

Lesson

I. POWER

"The gospel of Christ . . . is the power of God." The "good news" about Jesus Christ has power. The Greek word is *dunamis*, from which we get our word *dynamite*. The gospel of Christ carries with it the omnipotence of God, operative in regenerating a person.

4

A. The Dichotomy

    1. Man's desire

        Men would like to change. I believe that. All advertising that goes on in the world is based on one presupposition—that people want things different from the way they are. They want to look better, feel better, think better, have better experiences. They want to change their lives but, except from an external standpoint, are utterly impotent to do so.

    2. Man's deficiency

        a) His inability to change what he is

            Jeremiah 13:23 says, "Can the Ethiopian change his skin, or the leopard his spots?" We have just about as much chance to change our hearts. Aside from a few reformations here and there, men can't do a thing about what they are.

        b) His misunderstanding of what can change him

            "Ye do err, not knowing the scriptures, nor the power of God" (Matt. 22:29). That's what Jesus said to the religionists of His time, who, of all people, should have known God's power.

    3. God's deliverance

        The gospel of Jesus Christ has the power to change men and deliver them from sin, from Satan, from judgment, from death, and from hell.

        a) Acts 4:10*b*, 12—"By the name of Jesus Christ of Nazareth. . . . Neither is there salvation in any other; for there is no other name under heaven given among men, whereby we must be saved." Men believe they can be changed by being religious and doing good works. However, the Bible says only the power of God can change people.

        b) Romans 5:6—"For when we were yet without strength, in due time Christ died for the ungodly." Man was utterly trapped and unable to do a thing about his desperate condition.

        c) Romans 8:3—"For what the law could not do, in that it was weak through the flesh, God sending his own Son, . . . condemned sin in the flesh." In other words, you can give man good standards, good rules, and good principles, but he still can't change himself.

d) James 1:18a—"Of his own will begot he us with the word of truth." What man cannot do for himself, God can do for man.

e) 1 Peter 1:23—We have been "born again, not of corruptible seed [a human, decaying seed], but of incorruptible, by the word of God."

So God's Word can do for us what we cannot do for ourselves. Man is sinful and unable to remedy his condition, but from God comes the incredible, limitless power that can transform lives.

B. The Dilemma

1. 1 Corinthians 1:18—"For the preaching of the cross is to them that perish *foolishness*; but unto us who are saved it is the *power* of God" (italics added). A crucified Christ is just ridiculous to men.

2. 1 Corinthians 1:23-24—"But we preach Christ crucified, unto the Jews a stumbling block, and unto the Greeks foolishness; but unto them who are called, both Jews and Greeks, Christ [is] the power of God, and the wisdom of God."

He Who Laughs Last

The pagans in Rome and Corinth mocked the Christians. The gods of their religion were basically indifferent, apathetic, and remote. The idea of an incarnation of God was utterly ridiculous to them. An archaeological find from Rome, a caricature of the early Christian era, illustrates the attitude of the Romans toward Christianity at that time. It depicts a slave bowing down before a cross, upon which was crucified a jackass. The caption underneath the drawing mocked, "Alexamenos worships his god." They thought the idea of a crucified Christ was absolutely ridiculous. The world laughs at us—they mock us. But we know better.

3. 1 Corinthians 2:1-5—Paul is saying to the Corinthians, "I had one message when I came to you, and it was the very message you despised. Mock the cross if you will—it is still the power of God. So I preach the cross 'that your faith should not stand in the wisdom of men, but in the power of God' " (v. 5).

I have seen the message of the cross transform thousands of

people in my lifetime. Let the world say what it will, the evidence is in, and the cross transforms us. The power of God's kingdom is amazing. What's really incredible is, despite my own human limitations, God uses me as a channel, a tool to change people for time and eternity.

C. The Description

1. In the Old Testament

   In the Old Testament we see a manifold description of God's power as:

   a) Great power (Ps. 79:11)

   b) Strong power (Ps. 89:13)

   c) Glorious power (Ex. 15:6)

   d) Mighty power (Job 9:4)

   e) Everlasting power (Isa. 26:4)

   f) Sovereign power (Ex. 9:16)

   g) Effectual power (Isa. 43:13)

   h) Irresistible power (Deut. 32:39)

   i) Incomparable power (Ps. 89:8)

   j) Unsearchable power (Job 5:9)

   k) Creation power (Jer. 27:5)

   l) Salvation power (Ps. 106:8-9)

2. In the New Testament

   Behind each miracle in the Bible there is the power of God. God the Son, unto whom all power is given (Matt. 28:18), had the power to:

   a) Cast out demons (Mark 5:1-20)

   b) Heal every sickness (Luke 8:40-56)

   c) Provide for physical needs (Mark 6:30-34)

   d) Still the storm (Mark 4:35-41)

   e) Walk on the water (Mark 6:48-51)

   f) Raise the dead (Mark 5:22-43; Rom. 1:4)

   g) Save souls (Rom. 1:16)

      Most of all, "the gospel of Christ . . . is the power of God unto *salvation*" (italics added).

I really believe that the greatest expression of God's power is found in His power to save, to transform people, and to change their nature and their destiny.

7

II. SALVATION

"The gospel of Christ . . . is the power of God unto salvation."

A. Its Definition

   Salvation as a noun is used eighteen times by Paul, and as a verb, twenty-nine times. The power is seen in salvation because men, being spiritually dead, are made alive to live forever—cleansed from sin and fit for the kingdom by a saving act of God. What does *salvation* mean? It means "deliverance."

B. Its Dimension

   1. Present

      a) Salvation from life's infection

         We are saved from a crooked and perverse generation (Acts 2:40). This salvation from sin and Satan includes, on the positive side: forgiveness, life in the Spirit, and victory over trials (2 Pet. 1:3).

      b) Salvation from lostness

         "The Son of man is come to seek and to save that which was lost" (Luke 19:10). Man's on the wrong road, and he doesn't know where he's going, where he's coming from, or where he is. But when he comes to Christ, instantly he knows where he came from, where he's going, and right where he is. Jesus can give purpose, direction, and hope to a life of despair.

   2. Future

      a) Salvation from death and hell

         This is initiated by spiritual rebirth and consummated by physical resurrection (1 Pet. 1:3-4).

      b) Salvation from inevitable judgment by God's wrath

         As believers we are not destined for the wrath of God but for an entrance into eternal blessedness (1 Thess. 5:9).

C. Its Desire

   I believe that the culture in which Paul wrote was ready for this message. I think they were looking for salvation just as men are today. They may think they need economic salvation or political salvation or social salvation, or that they just need to upgrade their lives and their society—but they're looking for salvation.

8

D. Its Divine Necessity

    1. Man's condition

      The Bible characterizes man as:

      a) Grossly, willfully ignorant (Eph. 4:18)

      b) Purposefully self-indulgent and unwilling to forsake all (James 4:1; Luke 14:33)

      c) Steeped in false religion (Rom. 1:25)

      d) Filled with the wrong motives (James 4:3)

      e) Trusting in their own good deeds (Rom. 10:3)

      f) Loving the passing things of the world (James 4:4)

      g) Hating the truth (Rom. 1:25)

      h) Proudly independent and self-centered (Ps. 14:1)

      As such they have no right to enter the kingdom of God (cf. Luke 18:17, 25; 1 Cor. 6:9-10; Gal. 5:19*b*-21).

    2. God's provision

      Man is so lost, so infected, so doomed, and so dead in sin that it takes the power of God to deliver him from all of that. Through God's power, then, the gospel becomes active in the world to bring about man's deliverance from God's present and eternal wrath and man's reinstatement in that glory of God which was lost through sin.

So Paul's thesis is that the *power* of God can bring *salvation*. But how?

III. FAITH

"The gospel of Christ . . . is the power of God unto salvation to everyone that *believeth*; to the Jew first, and also to the Greek" (italics added). Salvation power operates only through faith—that's all. Where there is faith there is the power of God operative in salvation. You say, "What is faith?"

A. The Predicate of Faith

    Faith is believing. You live by faith every day of your life. You turn on your faucet, fill the glass, and drink it. That's faith. You don't know what's really in that water. Faith is trusting. You go to a restaurant, and you eat what they serve you. We all live by faith. That's the only way we can survive. God has put in the heart of man the understanding of living by faith. Though faith in the spiritual dimension is far different from that kind of faith, it is nonetheless the same idea of trusting and believing. But for salvation, what must we believe?

B. The Object of Faith

Romans 10:9 states: "If thou shalt confess with thy mouth the Lord Jesus, and shalt believe in thine heart that God hath raised him from the dead, thou shalt be saved." That means if you believe Christ is who He said He was, that He died for the reason He said He died, and that He rose again from the grave, you are a believer. The multitude came to Jesus and asked, "What shall we do, that we might work the works of God? Jesus answered, and said unto them, This is the work of God, that ye *believe on him* whom he hath sent" (John 6:28-29, italics added). God asks men to believe in Christ.

1. Replaced

Many people think they're saved for the wrong reasons. They replace the intended object of true faith with substitutes that are powerless to save. Faith resulting in salvation is not:

   a) Professing Christianity

   b) Being baptized

   c) Going to church

   d) Reforming your morals

   e) Conforming to rules

   f) Using self-discipline and restraint

2. Recognized

Salvation comes because a man or a woman recognizes that he or she has no resources and is lost, due to the filthiness and deformity of their sin. When one perceives the rottenness of his heart and the pollution of his nature, he is drawn to Christ as a remedy. He sees the One who died for his sin, who conquered his sin and paid the price that he might have new life, and he says, "I believe!"

C. The Subjects of Faith

As we saw in verse 16, salvation by faith is for "everyone that believeth; to the Jew first, and also to the Greek" (v. 16c). Salvation is available to everyone who believes. Let's face it, from a Jewish perspective you are either a Jew or a Greek (i.e., Gentile; non-Jew). There are no other kinds of people. Salvation was first extended to the Jews since they were

God's specially chosen people. It is to the Jew first that Jesus, the Messiah, came. He said, "I am not sent but unto the lost sheep of the house of Israel" (Matt. 15:24; cf. Matt. 10:6).

Thus, although Jews and Gentiles were united in the participation of the gospel, the Jews were not deprived of their distinguished rank—they were called first. Salvation was offered first to the Jew but then also to the Gentile. God's salvation is not limited to any nation (Gen. 12:3) but is offered and is to be preached to everyone, whether Jew or Gentile.

We have seen that the gospel of Christ has power to save everyone who believes. But how can it, even if he believes? How can it change him?

IV. RIGHTEOUSNESS

"For in it is the righteousness of God revealed."

A. Activated

The reason the gospel of Christ can save is that when you believe, the righteousness of God is revealed to you. In other words, it becomes yours. You say, "Man is so sinful, so evil, so hopeless, so helpless, that even if he believed, and even if it has the power to save, how can it?" It cannot save because we all of a sudden become righteous but because all of a sudden to us is revealed the righteousness of God; or better yet, the righteousness *from* God. When Paul says the righteousness of God is revealed, he doesn't mean it's just disclosed to human minds or just spoken in history. He means that it is specifically revealed in the action and operation of regeneration. That is why "the gospel . . . is the power of God unto salvation to everyone that believeth" (v. 16*b*); that belief activates the righteousness from God, which is imparted to the believer.

B. Imparted

If I am to be righteous, God must give me His righteousness, for I have none of my own. Even if I believe, I can't be righteous in myself, perfectly holy, or without sin by God's standards. You see, Jesus took our sin, our absolute inability to be righteous, and, in exchange, God gave us His righteousness.

Why God Demands the Impossible

God demands from man absolute, perfect holiness. Some people think that might be unjust, so they ask, "How could God demand that? Why doesn't He lower the standard?" Well, let's say He did lower the standard a little bit and said, "In order to be saved you have to be highly intelligent." Would that be fair? No, it would be unjust to those without intelligence. If He said, "You have to be rich," that would be unjust to poor people. He set a standard that nobody could qualify for, so that nobody can boast and nobody needs to be left out.

1. 2 Corinthians 5:21—"For he [God] hath made him [Christ], who knew no sin, to be sin for us, that we might be made the rightousness of God in him."

2. Romans 3:21a, 22—"But now the righteousness of God apart from the law is manifested." How? "Even the righteousness of God which is by faith of Jesus Christ unto all and upon all them that believe."

3. Romans 4:3—"For what saith the scripture? Abraham believed God, and it was counted unto him for righteousness."

4. Philippians 3:8b-9—Paul says, "I have suffered the loss of all things, and do count them but refuse, that I may win Christ, and be found in him, not having mine own righteousness, which is of the law, but that which is through the faith of Christ, the righteousness which is of God by faith."

5. Romans 1:17—"For in it [the gospel] is the righteousness of God revealed from faith to faith; as it is written, the just shall live by faith"(cf. Hab. 2:4). "Faith to faith" has the same idea as "to everyone that believeth" (v. 16b). The righteousness of God is revealed from faith to faith: this person's faith, that person's faith, anyone's faith—with no limitations.

The just, down through the ages, have always lived by faith in the One who alone has the righteousness to impart to men—righteousness that can secure their salvation. I hope you have responded to this transforming power of God by trusting Christ to provide His righteousness on your behalf.

Focusing on the Facts

1. What two verses in chapter 1 form the theme for the book of Romans (see p. 2)?
2. The apostle Paul was not ashamed of the gospel. What did he endure as a result (see pp. 2-3)?

12

3. Why do we tend to be silent about the gospel when we should speak (see p. 3)?
4. Explain the philosophy of the health and wealth movement in American Christianity (see p. 3).
5. Name two things that keep men from Christ (see p. 4).
6. Why was Paul so bold in preaching the gospel, according to Romans 1:16 (see p. 4)?
7. What was Paul's supreme passion? Cite a Bible verse to support your answer (see p. 4).
8. What kind of power does the gospel have (see p. 4)?
9. How do many people believe they can be changed (see pp. 4-5)?
10. Cite a verse that states how God's Word can transform lives (see pp. 5-6).
11. What does the preaching of the cross seem to unbelievers (1 Cor. 1:18; see p. 6)?
12. What is perhaps the greatest expression of God's power (see p. 7)?
13. Describe the present and future dimensions of salvation (see p. 8).
14. What does the gospel deliver men from (see p. 8)?
15. Describe faith (see pp. 9-10).
16. Identify the object of the Christian faith. Support your answer with Scripture (see p. 10).
17. List some of the substitutes people come up with for the true object of faith (see p. 10).
18. What must a person recognize about himself before he can be saved (see p. 10)?
19. To whom is salvation available? To whom was it first made available (Rom. 1:16; see pp. 10-11)?
20. What does the gospel impart to the believer? Explain (see p. 11).
21. Why does God demand an impossible standard (see p. 12)?

Pondering the Principles

1. Have you been influenced by those who have compromised the message of Christianity by emphasizing health and wealth? Contrary to what some religious leaders would have you believe, Christ never set comfort or riches as goals for those who follow Him. Read Matthew 6:19-24; 13:22; 19:21-24; and Luke 12:13-21. What warnings did Jesus give in those verses about acquiring riches? Now read Matthew 10:34-37, Luke 9:23-27, and John 15:18-21. What type of conditions could the followers of Christ expect to encounter? What are the dangers of pursuing riches and personal comfort as ends in themselves? Do you need to be

weaned away from material, temporal things and be nourished upon spiritual, eternal things? Where are you storing your treasure?

2. Do you truly understand the greatness of divine power that is channeled through God's Word? When you do, you will be ready to share the gospel with anyone who will listen. Often we can be intimidated from telling others about Christ because spiritual things seem so foolish to a society that exalts the power of man's technology. But we forget that the gospel transforms lives. Consider the effects Paul's preaching had on the Thessalonians in 1 Thessalonians 1:6—2:13. Commit yourself to speaking boldly for God, not being concerned about "pleasing men but God, who examines our hearts" (1 Thess. 2:4; NASB).

3. Do you have friends or neighbors who do not trust in Christ for their salvation? Ask them if they know what the Bible says about eternal life and find out what they are trusting for it. Ask them if they agree it is possible for even a religious person to be confused about the proper object of faith. Tell them of the confusion of a Jewish religious leader in John 3 named Nicodemus. Show them that Christ is the only worthy object of faith by explaining such verses as John 3:15-16, 36 and John 6:40. Conclude by taking them to Philippians 3:8-9 to reveal what faith in Christ offers that we can't obtain for ourselves.

4. In His justice, God wisely set a standard no one can qualify for. Praise Him that it is met when He imputes the righteousness of Christ to those who believe in Him. Meditate on Romans 5:12-21.

2
The Wrath of God

Outline

Introduction
A. The Preparation for God's Wrath
B. The Perspective of God's Wrath
C. The Prominence of God's Wrath
   1. In the Old Testament
   2. In the New Testament
D. The Penalty of God's Wrath

Lesson
I. The Quality of Wrath
  A. Unlike Man's
  B. Unique to God
    1. God's Holiness
      a) Habakkuk 1:13*a*
      b) John 2:13-17
    2. God's Justice
      a) Lamentations 1:18*a*
      b) Joshua 7
II. The Time of Wrath
  A. Defined
  B. Demonstrated
  C. Delayed
III. The Source of Wrath
  A. Moral Order
    1. The physical laws
      a) The law of gravity
      b) The laws of force and acceleration
    2. The Moral Laws
  B. Personal Action
    1. Explained
    2. Expressed

Introduction

We have seen that Romans 1:16-17 has served as Paul's theme or thesis of the entire epistle to the Romans. Moving now to verse 18, Paul is beginning to unfold the substance of the theme so that we might understand the significance and meaning of the fullness of the gospel of Christ.

A. The Preparation for God's Wrath

The gospel message begins with a statement about the wrath of God: "For the wrath of God is revealed from heaven against all ungodliness and unrighteousness of men, who hold the truth in unrighteousness" (v. 18). In contrast to much of the contemporary evangelism that avoids the issue of judgment, Paul sees fear as the first pressure to be applied to evil men. Admittedly, the wrath of God is a hard subject to begin with when speaking to people about Christ; yet it is the beginning of the gospel and the proper preparation for the announcement of grace.

B. The Perspective of God's Wrath

People cannot fully understand God's love without also understanding God's hate; or His grace without knowing about His law; or comprehend His forgiveness until they understand the penalty for sin. Unless men sense that they are in grave danger of God's wrath, there is no pressure applied to them to change.

A look at one of God's other attributes, love, is necessary to better understand His wrath in the perspective. If God did not have wrath and anger, then He would not be God. God is perfect in love, on the one hand, and He is equally perfect in hate, on the other. Just as totally as He loves, so totally does He hate. Of Christ, Hebrews 1:9a says, "Thou hast loved righteousness, and hated iniquity." If you understand that God hates sin profoundly, then you will find it all the more amazing that He can love sinners. So without an understanding of His hate, His love is crippled also in our thinking. *Love* and *grace* are favorite terms, yet they are void of meaning if God does not hate.

C. The Prominence of God's Wrath

In spite of our aversion to seeing God as a God of hate and a God of wrath, the Scriptures clearly emphasize this.

1. In the Old Testament

a) Psalm 2:1-5, 12a—"Why do the nations rage, and the people imagine a vain thing? The kings of the earth set themselves, *and* the rulers take counsel together, against the Lord, and against his anointed, saying, Let us break their bonds asunder, and cast away their cords from us. He who sitteth in the heavens shall laugh; the Lord shall have them in derision. Then shall he speak unto them in his wrath, and vex them in his great displeasure. . . . Kiss the Son, lest he be angry, and ye perish from the way, when his wrath is kindled but a little."

b) Psalm 76:6-9a—"At thy rebuke, O God of Jacob, both the chariot and horse are cast into a dead sleep. Thou, even thou, art to be feared. And who may stand in thy sight when once thou art angry? Thou didst cause judgment to be heard from heaven; the earth feared, and was still, when God arose to judgment."

c) Psalm 90:7, 11—"For we are consumed by thine anger, and by thy wrath are we troubled. . . . Who knoweth the power of thine anger? Even according to thy fear, so is thy wrath."

d) Isaiah 9:19a—"Through the wrath of the Lord of hosts is the land darkened, and the people shall be as the fuel of the fire."

e) Jeremiah 7:20—"Therefore, thus saith the Lord God, Behold, mine anger and my fury shall be poured out upon this place, upon man, and upon beast, and upon the trees of the field, and upon the fruit of the ground; and it shall burn, and shall not be quenched."

f) Ezekiel 7:19b—"Their silver and their gold shall not be able to deliver them in the day of the wrath of the Lord; they shall not satisfy their souls, neither fill their stomachs, because it is the stumbling block of their iniquity."

Other examples in the Old Testament show the wrath of God directed against: the old world in the Flood (Gen. 6-7); the people at the tower of Babel (Gen. 11); the cities of Sodom and Gomorrah and the plain (Gen. 19); the Egyptians (Ex. 5-14); the Israelites (Ex. 32: Lev. 10; Num. 12-14); and the enemies of Israel (2 Chron. 32).

2. In the New Testament

a) John 3:36—"He that believeth on the Son hath everlasting life; and he that believeth not the Son shall not see life, but the wrath of God abideth on him."

b) Romans 9:22—"What if God, willing to show his wrath and to make his power known, endured with much longsuffering the vessels of wrath fitted to destruction?"

c) Ephesians 5:6—"Let no man deceive you with vain words; for because of these things cometh the wrath of God upon the sons of disobedience."

d) 2 Thessalonians 1:7b-9—"The Lord Jesus shall be revealed from heaven with his mighty angels, in flaming fire taking vengeance on them that know not God, and that obey not the gospel of our Lord Jesus Christ; who shall be punished with everlasting destruction from the presence of the Lord, and from the glory of his power."

God is a God of wrath. He's a God of anger. Now does that sound like a poor choice of starting points for the gospel? Doesn't the bad news have to come before the good news? Just as the good news of a cure to a disease that has been diagnosed as fatal is gratefully welcomed, so also does the reality of God's loving salvation take on a like meaning when it is preceded by the diagnosis of the bad news—God hates our sin, which leads us toward death.

18

D. The Penalty of God's Wrath

The "for" at the beginning of verse 18 connects this verse to the idea of justification by faith alone, mentioned in the previous passage. This verse is saying that all men unrighteously hold the truth and are under the wrath of God; therefore, they have no capacity to justify themselves. So justification has to be by faith, because all men, left to their own efforts, are under the wrath. Paul says in Romans 3:23, "For all have sinned, and come short of the glory of God." He continues this idea in Ephesians 2:1-3: "And you hath he made alive, who were dead in trespasses and sins; in which in times past ye walked according to the course of this world, according to the prince of the power of the air, the spirit that now worketh in the sons of disobedience; among whom also we all had our manner of life in times past in the lusts of our flesh, fulfilling the desires of the flesh and of the mind, and were by nature the children of wrath, even as others." Everyone born into this world is a spiritually dead "child of wrath," who is a victim of lust and desire to do evil. The sentence has already been passed—the whole human race is damned to hell as children of wrath under the judgment of God.

Six features of wrath are presented here in verse 18.

Lesson

I. THE QUALITY OF WRATH

"For the wrath of God."

A. Unlike Man's

The wrath of God is *divine* wrath, and that is a very important beginning. It is not like your wrath or my wrath. We get angry when we are offended; pride gets in the way. The passion that we call anger in this human world is always reflective of the evil heart of man. Even in this warped world, indignation against wickedness is an essential of human goodness. We expect people to get angry about obvious injustice, yet, even when we are angry about the right things, that anger is usually polluted by our sinfulness. But we must not push our concept of anger off onto God. God's anger is not some capriciously selfish and irrational rage.

19

B. Unique to God

The absolute, perfect quality of God's wrath is related to the following attributes of God:

1. God's holiness

   Like every other attribute of God, His wrath is as perfect as His holy person. In fact, God could not be God, and be holy, if He didn't react to evil. For God to be God, His holiness demands that He not tolerate unholiness.

   a) Habakkuk 1:13a—Habakkuk, the prophet, knew of God's holiness; that's why he said, "Thou art of purer eyes than to behold evil, and canst not look on iniquity."

   The more Godlike you become, the more angry you will get about things that are an affront to God's holy character (e.g., Ps. 69:9; Acts 8:14-24; Eph. 4:26-27).

   b) John 2:13-17—A classic illustration of holy wrath is when Jesus cleansed the Temple by making a whip and driving out the people and animals and overturning the tables. Did you know that this dramatic scene was His first public act in Jerusalem? That's not exactly the way you start a crusade, but Jesus was furious because God was being dishonored.

2. God's justice

   The wrath of God is always perfect—always.

   a) Lamentations 1:18a—"The Lord is righteous; for I have rebelled against his commandment. Hear, I pray you, all people, and behold my sorrow." In other words, "God is judging me but it's all right—I deserve it, for He is righteous.

   b) Joshua 7—Remember what happened to Achan? God told Israel not to steal anything from Jericho, but Achan disobeyed and hid some stolen goods from Jericho under his tent. Joshua, finding that Achan was guilty, said to him, "Confess your sin and give glory to God" (v. 19). Did Joshua mean that God was going to "let him off the hook" if he confessed? No, because he and his family, who must have been implicated in the whole operation, were put to death by God's instruction. Instead, Joshua was saying, "Before you get your due judgment from God, confess your sin—say you're guilty, and that what God does to you is the proper reaction of His holiness." In other words, don't you *ever* impugn God as if He did something impure! Even when God is angry it is the right expression of His utter holiness.

So we see that the quality of God's wrath is holy and just, in accordance with His perfect character. God doesn't "blow His cork" or "fly off the handle" in a momentary fury (Gk., *thumos*). The wrath of God is, rather, a settled indignation (Gk., *orgē*) by One who could never be good and loving unless He totally hated evil. God's love and God's wrath are inseparable.

II. THE TIME OF WRATH

"For the wrath of God is revealed."

A. Defined

What does Paul mean by "is revealed"? The literal rendering reads "is constantly being revealed." Therefore, the temporal aspect of God's wrath is that it's constantly being revealed (Gk., *apokaluptō*), "brought to light, uncovered, made manifest or known." God's wrath is always being made known.

B. Demonstrated

God's wrath has been visible in all of human history. It was revealed in:

1. The Garden (Gen. 3:14-19)

   Adam and Eve sinned, and the sentence of death was passed, the earth was cursed, and they were thrown out of paradise. This was the world's great beginning lesson on the fact that God hates sin.

2. The Flood (Gen. 6:5-17)

   God drowned the entire evil human race except for eight faithful souls.

3. The destruction of Sodom and Gomorrah (Gen. 19)

4. The curse of the law upon every transgressor (Gal. 3:10)

5. The institution of the sacrificial system (Heb. 9:19-22)

6. The subjection of creation to the curse (Rom. 8:19-22; cf. Gen. 3:17)

7. The suffering and crucifixion of Christ (Gal. 3:13)

Above all, I believe the greatest demonstration of the wrath of God was given on Calvary's cross. God hates sin so deeply that He poured out His fury on His own beloved Son.

21

C. Delayed

You say to yourself, "Now wait a minute, there are some people who seem to prosper in spite of God's wrath against ungodliness and unrighteousness. How can such men live and get away with it?" Well, don't forget Psalm 9:16a, which says, "The Lord is known by the judgment which he executeth." Judgment will come. If God lets men prosper for a while in their sin, it's just that His bowl of wrath is all the while being filled up and His sword sharpened. The longer God pulls back the bow, the deeper the arrow plunges when He releases it. Remember, God does not settle all His accounts at the same time (Ps. 7:12-13; 10; 37:1-15; 73:10-20).

III. THE SOURCE OF WRATH

"For the wrath of God is revealed from heaven."

Where is the source of this wrath? It is revealed from the throne of God and is effectively operative in the world of men in basically two ways:

A. Moral Order

1. The physical laws

   When God made the world He built into it certain laws— and when they are broken, there are consequences.

   a) The law of gravity—If you climb a tall building and jump off, it doesn't matter what you want to do—you will go down.

   b) The laws of force and acceleration—If you drive into a concrete wall at eighty miles an hour, you become an irresistible force plunging into an immovable object.

2. The moral laws

   God has built into the spiritual world moral laws of consequence. In this regard Paul speaks of God's wrath in an almost impersonal sense.

   a) Romans 3:5—God brings on men *the* wrath.

   b) Romans 5:9—The justified are saved from *the* wrath.

   c) Romans 12:19—Believers are to leave vengeance upon evildoers to *the* wrath.

   d) Romans 13:5—A motive for obedience is *the* wrath.

e) 1 Thessalonians 1:10—The Lord will deliver believers from *the* wrath.

Note that in the Greek text the definite article (translated "the" in English) appears before the word "wrath" in each of these verses.

There are inevitable consequences for violating God's moral order. If you do things that are immoral, you will pay a price.

B. Personal Action

1. Explained

God is not a cosmic force who made laws and let them run their course; His wrath is not automatic judgment by an anonymous cosmic computer. God is involved, and the Bible shows a very intense personal reaction to sin within the heart of the divine being.

Let's look at some of the terms in the Old Testament that speak of God's reaction of anger.

a) *Charah*—used ninety-two times and commonly of God. It means "to become heated up, to burn with fury."

b) *Chârôn*—used forty-one times. It refers exclusively to divine anger and means "a burning, fierce wrath" (e.g., Ex. 32:12).

c) *Qâtsaph*—Used thirty-four times, and eighteen of those refer to God. It means "to be bitter."

d) *Chêmâh*—used mostly of God. It refers to a venom or a poison and is frequently associated with jealousy (e.g., Nah. 1:2).

2. Expressed

Psalm 7:11 says, "God judgeth the righteous, and God is angry with the wicked every day." This anger is expressed by the term *za'am*, which carries with it the idea that God is so furious it is as if He foams at the mouth. There is moral law and order, but there is also the personal act of God as He expresses the wrath of a holy nature—a wrath that comes from heaven because God has established the moral order, and He reacts in a holy anger to the ungodliness and unrighteousness of men.

IV. THE NATURE OF WRATH

"For the wrath of God is revealed from heaven against all ungodliness and unrighteousness of men."

The nature of wrath is seen in that it is directed "against all ungodliness and unrighteousness of men." His wrath is against sin; and as we've just seen, it's not the uncontrolled irrational fury of a criminal who might take his vengeance out on the nearest person, but rather it is discriminatingly and carefully pointed at the ungodliness and unrighteousness of men. What do the words *ungodliness* and *unrighteousness* tell us? Though they overlap in their definitions and basically add emphasis to God's anger over sin, these terms have some interesting shades of meaning:

A. Ungodliness (Gk., *asebeia*)

Asebeia focuses on man's relationship to God. God is angry because men are not rightly related to Him. The ungodliness of men is evidenced by their impiety toward God—their lack of reverence, devotion, and worship of Him, which leads to idolatry. (Note the four "ungodlies" of Jude 15; cf. 2 Tim. 2:16; Titus 2:12; 1 Pet. 4:18; 2 Pet. 2:5-6; 3:7.)

B. Unrighteousness (Gk., *adikia*)

While *adikia* encompasses the first concept as well, it emphasizes more the result of *asebeia*. When you are not rightly related to God and fail to reverence Him properly, then your transactions with everyone else around you aren't right either. All sin, you see, first attacks God's majesty and then His law. Men treat other men unrighteously because they treat God that way. When man becomes unrelated to God, his human relationships and transactions become corrupted. Ungodliness leads to unrighteousness; and such a failure to reverence God's laws leads to immorality (cf. Rom. 6:13; 2 Thess. 2:12; 2 Pet. 2:13, 15; 1 John 5:17).

The Only Thing God Hates

The only thing God hates is *sin*. Did you know that? He doesn't hate poor people or dumb people or smart people. He doesn't hate anybody. God just hates sin. It's the one thing that will keep any man from entering His presence (cf. Hab. 1:13; Heb. 12:14; Rev. 21:10, 27).

V. THE EXTENT OF WRATH

"For the wrath of God is revealed from heaven against all ungodliness and unrighteousness of men."

You might say, "Well, I'm a pretty good guy. You can't be talking about me, MacArthur, because I belong to the Royal Order of the Goats, I give to charity, and I'm basically a good person." But what does verse 18 say? "For the wrath of God is revealed from heaven against *all* ungodliness" (italics added). Likewise, in Romans 3:23, "For *all* have sinned, and come short of the glory of God" (italics added). Sure, some people are better than others, humanly speaking, but no one can meet the demands of a holy God.

For the sake of illustration, let's compare the attempt of sinful men to reach a holy God with the attempt to jump twenty-six miles from a Southern California beach out to the island of Catalina. We'll give you a running start, and you can run as fast and as long as you want before you jump. Some might get about six feet out and others maybe twenty-six feet, but no one would make it there. Regardless of man's individual differences, it's still too far to jump.

It's the same in the spiritual realm. I don't care who you are; the faintest trace of ungodliness and unrighteousness brings you under the wrath of God, from which no one can escape (cf. Ezek. 17:11-24).

You may say, "How can God hold all these poor people responsible? I was born into a sinful family just like everyone else. What do I know?" You'd be surprised what you know. At the end of verse 18 Paul identifies the real problem.

VI. THE CAUSE OF WRATH

"For the wrath of God is revealed from heaven against all ungodliness and unrighteousness of men, who hold the truth in unrighteousness."

Literally we would read the Greek text this way: "Men, who are constantly attempting to suppress the truth by their sin."

A. Suppression of the Truth

1. Truth is assaulted

Sin is in the heart of man so strongly that it assaults the truth. The fundamental truth of God and His Word is always assaulted by sin. There's always been an attempt to suppress it, to bury it, to obliterate it. Ironically, however, in spite of their futile attempts, men themselves become assaulted by the truth with guilt.

2. Truth is available

People often ask, "What about the heathen who have never heard about the true God?" The truth *is* there, but men suppress it. I really believe that God has revealed Himself to every individual. And if individuals, wherever they are and no matter how remote they are, do not suppress the truth that is available to them, then that truth can lead them away from the excesses of sin to the saving truth of God by His gracious providence. All men possess enough seeds of divine truth to ultimately preserve them from hell, but they've halted the growth of those seeds by their love of sin.

3. Truth is avoided

    a) John 3:19-20—"Men loved darkness rather than light." But why? "Because their deeds were evil" (v. 19*b*).

    b) Psalm 14:1—"The fool hath said in his heart, There is no God." Why? We see it here again: because "they are corrupt, they have done abominable works, there is none that doeth good." Sinful man doesn't want a God to call him into accountability. So he either postulates that no God exists or he invents a god who can tolerate his sin. Thus, he clearly avoids the true voice of God, and the wrath of God still waits.

B. Suspension of Wrath

Commentator Donald Grey Barnhouse illustrates the wrath that has been waiting as a great water that has been accumulating behind the dam of God's patience (*Romans*, vol. 1 [Grand Rapids: Eerdmans, 1953], pp. 227-28). The wrath of God against every sin—past, present, or future—is stored up, waiting for the day when His patience shall burst into its holy end. Though for the most part, God seemed to overlook the sins of man in the centuries before the cross, His wrath was in reality just piling up.

C. Substitution of Christ

That dam broke one day, and it broke at Calvary. It broke on Christ and drowned Him in all the sea of sin, and it will break again and drown all those who are not in Christ. He took the judgment in place of those who have trusted in Him. Those who do not believe will take their own judgment. The wrath of God awaits them because they hold the truth, and, no matter what they claim, they hold it and suppress it because of their sin.

So the wrath of God is where the gospel begins. But remember, there is good news. And the good news is that Christ has taken the full fury of God's wrath for everyone, if you'll accept His gracious substitution for you.

Focusing on the Facts

1. What element does contemporary evangelism often avoid? What is the proper preparation for announcing the grace of God (see p. 16)?
2. What did God direct His wrath against in the Old Testament (see pp. 17-18)?
3. What will happen to those who do not know God and do not obey the gospel when Christ returns from heaven (2 Thess. 1:7-9; see p. 18)?
4. In what spiritual condition is everyone born into the world (see p. 19)?
5. What sentence has already been passed on the human race (see p. 19)?
6. How is human anger unlike God's wrath (see p. 19)?
7. What two attributes of God are related to His wrath? Explain (see pp. 20-21).
8. What kind of things should anger a Christian who becomes more Godlike in his character (see p. 20)?
9. What was the first public act of Jesus' ministry in Jerusalem (John 2:13-17)? Why did He react as He did (see p. 20)?
10. Did Achan's confession of his sin keep him from being punished? Explain (see pp. 20-21).
11. Where was the greatest demonstration of God's wrath given (see pp. 21-22)?
12. When God does not immediately react against men's unrighteousness, does that mean He has let them off the hook? Explain (see p. 22).
13. How has God demonstrated His wrath in an impersonal sense? What do the Hebrew words used for God's anger show about His reaction to sin (see pp. 22-23)?
14. What is God's anger directed against, according to Romans 1:18? What is the one thing that will keep any man from entering God's presence (see p. 24)?
15. Is anyone exempt from God's wrath? Why? Support your answer with Scripture (see pp. 24-25).
16. What does man attempt to suppress in his unrighteousness (Rom. 1:18; see p. 25)?
17. How can people even in remote areas be led away from the excesses of sin to salvation (see pp. 25-26)?

18. What does sinful man do to avoid being called to divine account-ability (see p. 26)?
19. Upon whom will the dam of God's wrath break in the future (see p. 26)?
20. What is the good news about God's wrath (see pp. 26-27)?

Pondering the Principles

1. When you get angry, is it for the right reasons? Or is it because you have been offended or inconvenienced? Pride is often the main cause for anger. The next time you are angry, ask the Spirit to fill you with gentleness, patience, and self-control as you evaluate the cause of your anger (Gal. 5:22-23). Ephesians 4:26-27 says, "'In your anger do not sin': Do not let the sun go down while you are still angry, and do not give the devil a foothold" (NIV; cf. 2 Cor. 2:10-11). Unless your anger is a controlled, selfless reaction over something that grieves God and hinders His cause, immediately confess it as unjustified. If you don't, that unresolved source of conflict may fester into a divisive situation that will destroy the unity and peace God desires every Christian to experience (Eph. 4:3).

2. Is God's holiness and justice the foundation of your witnessing to others about Christ? Without that foundation, the concepts of man's sin and Christ's sacrifice have little meaning. Make verses like John 3:36 and 2 Thessalonians 1:7-9 a part of your gospel presentation.

3. Do you let the prosperity of unspiritual and unbelieving people distract you from your own commitment to godliness? Do you believe that God will always materially prosper you in your pursuit of godliness? Beware of doing something godly so you can receive a material reward. That will pervert your motive for righteous living. Meditate on Psalm 73, recognizing that tempo-ral, material prosperity is no indicator of divine blessing.

4. Praise God that Jesus took the wrath of God on Himself at the cross so you would never have to experience it. Consider communicating how Jesus died in Barabbas's place (Luke 23:13-25) as a graphic way to reinforce that fact. Tell unbelievers how Jesus has already died in their place, allowing them to escape God's wrath if they will believe in Christ and follow Him.

3
Reasons for the Wrath of God— Part 1

Outline

Introduction
A. The Reality of Judgment Denied
B. The Reality of Judgment Depicted
   1. By Jesus
   2. By Paul
C. The Reality of Judgment Demonstrated
   1. By great men of God
   2. By worshipers of false gods
      a) Their remembrance
      b) Their reversal
      c) Their retribution
      d) Their repentance
D. The Reality of Judgment Deserved

Lesson
I. Revelation (vv. 19-20)
   A. Its Communication to All Men
   B. Its Content Concerning God's Nature
      1. His goodness
      2. His sovereignty
      3. His eternal power and Godhead
   C. Its Clarity in What Is Seen
      1. In ancient times
      2. In modern times
         a) Zoology
            (1) Migration
            (2) Aviation
            (3) Protection
         b) Meteorology
         c) Astronomy

(1) The earth
(2) Comets
(3) The sun
(4) The Milky Way

Conclusion

Introduction

In the last lesson, we saw that all men stand in condemnation before God. His judgment is certain and inevitable—no man can escape. To set the stage for understanding the reasons for God's wrath, we need to first investigate the reality of judgment.

A. The Reality of Judgment Denied

Some years ago, the head of the Department of Evangelism for one of the largest denominations in America said this: "We don't need to evangelize the people of the world who have never heard the message of salvation; we only need to announce to them that they are already saved."

Today in Christianity there is a rising trend in what is called "universalism." This is the belief that ultimately everybody will be saved because God is too kind, too gracious, and too good to cast people into an eternal hell. Universalism would have us believe that we shouldn't be concerned about judgment or hell and that consequently we needn't worry about Christ's command "Go ye into all the world, and preach the gospel to every creature" (Mark 16:15b). Reasoning that the people who have never heard the gospel can't be responsible for what they don't know, this unbiblical system of thought would encourage us to leave the unevangelized people alone, since it believes everybody will go to heaven anyway.

B. The Reality of Judgment Depicted

1. By Jesus

Universalism is not the view of the Lord, who said, "The harvest truly is plenteous, but the laborers are few. Pray ye, therefore, the Lord of the harvest, that he will send forth laborers into his harvest" (Matt. 9:37b-38). This harvest of which Jesus spoke is a harvest of judgment. Seeing humanity as a mass of people about to be cut off and judged, the need for laborers to enter the harvest to warn them was of vital concern to Him. In fact, if we look at the whole context of Scripture, not only do we see the

30

Lord speaking about hell more than anyone else in the entire Bible but also more than everyone else put together in the New Testament.

2. By Paul

The apostle Paul said, "Knowing, therefore, the terror of the Lord, we persuade men" (2 Cor. 5:11a). In other words, it is because of the terror of God's judgment that we should be motivated to evangelize.

C. The Reality of Judgment Demonstrated

1. By great men of God

a) John Knox (sixteenth-century Scottish reformer)—On his knees for lost souls in Scotland, he pleaded with God, "Give me Scotland or I die."

b) Hudson Taylor (nineteenth-century English founder of the China Inland Mission)—As a young man he looked across the thousands of miles to the unreached multitudes of China and cried out to God, "I feel that I cannot go on living unless I do something for the lost in China."

c) Henry Martyn (eighteenth-century English missionary to India and Persia)—After landing in India he said, "Here I am in the midst of heathen midnight and savage oppression. Now, my dear Lord, let me burn out for Thee."

d) James Chalmers (nineteenth-century Scottish missionary to the South Sea Islands)—So concerned was this missionary for those without the Savior that it is said of him, "In Christ's service he joyfully endured hardness, hunger, shipwreck, and exhausting toil. He risked his life a thousand times and was finally clubbed to death, beheaded, and eaten by men whom he sought to enlighten."

e) Robert Arthington (nineteenth-century English businessman from a wealthy family)—Unable himself to go overseas, he enabled others to reach the lost by living meagerly while sacrificially giving over $500,000 to foreign missions. He wrote, "Gladly would I make the floor my bed, a box my chair, and another box my table, rather than that men should perish for the want of the knowledge of Christ."

These men understood what it means to die without God

and Christ. They understood that men are under the wrath of God and are inevitably headed toward judgment. As we have seen in the previous lesson, this is precisely the point Paul was making when he wrote, "For the wrath of God is revealed from heaven against all ungodliness and unrighteousness of men, who hold the truth in unrighteousness" (Rom. 1:18).

2. By worshipers of false gods

Some men through the history of the world have recognized the reality of judgment and God's right to be angry with them. Let me give you an illustration from 1 Samuel, chapters 4 through 6:

At this particular time in the history of Israel, the nation was paying no attention to God. There was a bit of religious tokenism, but no genuineness. Having just lost a battle against their perennial enemy, the Philistines, Israel sent to Shiloh to get the Ark of the Covenant, over which the divine presence dwelt. Not wanting to lose another battle, Israel made plans to use the presence of God with the Ark to gain them victory. Now to the pagans this was just another idol, but in the Israelites' eyes, they had God. "And when the ark of the covenant of the Lord came into the camp, all Israel shouted with a great shout, so that the earth rang again" (4:5).

Now, despite the Philistines' worship of false gods, let's look at their reaction to the presence of the *true* God.

a) Their remembrance

While Israel was confidently shouting, "The day is won! God is here!" the Philistines were getting a little concerned: "And when the Philistines heard the noise of the shout, they said, What meaneth the noise of this great shout in the camp of the Hebrews? And they understood that the ark of the Lord was come into the camp. And the Philistines were afraid; for they said, God is come into the camp. And they said, Woe unto us! For there hath not been such a thing heretofore. Woe unto us! Who shall deliver us out of the hand of these mighty gods?" (4:6-8*a*). The Philistines were rightly afraid, because they remembered a little of Egyptian history: "These are the gods that smote the Egyptians with all the plagues" (4:8*b*).

b) Their reversal

After a brief pep talk, the Philistines decided to go into battle against Israel anyhow. Ironically, however, the Philistines were victorious, killing 30,000 of Israel's soldiers and capturing the Ark!

Now wait a minute. That's not the way the script is supposed to read. The Israelites were supposed to win—they had God! But God is not a utilitarian genie. You don't just rub your little lamp and say, "Now, God, go do Your thing—I'm in trouble. I know I haven't paid any attention to You for a long time, but I need You now." God doesn't operate like that, and the Israelites found that out.

Now if you think the Israelites had problems, having lost the battle and the Ark, you haven't begun to imagine what kind of problems the Philistines were going to have now that they had God on their hands.

c) Their retribution

The Ark was taken to Ashdod and placed in the pagan temple that housed the Philistine idol of one of their gods, Dagon. However, the true God made it known that He would tolerate no competition, for He did not allow the idol to stand in the presence of the Ark.

Furthermore, God's judgment fell upon the Philistines themselves; many were destroyed by a plague from mice and were afflicted with internal tumors. Obviously, the people of Ashdod knew where judgment was coming from: "The ark of the God of Israel shall not abide with us; for His hand is heavy upon us, and upon Dagon our god" (5:7*b*). Desiring to put an end to God's judgment upon them, they sent the Ark to Gath, and in turn, the Gathites dumped their problems upon the city of Ekron.

d) Their repentance

In deciding what to do with the Ark, the Philistines gathered together their diviners and priests: "And they said, If ye send away the ark of the God of Israel, send it not empty; but by all means return him a trespass offering" (6:3*a*). In other words, they were saying, "We acknowledge our sin: We have dishonored You. We deserve exactly what we have been

33

getting." Even these pagans understood that God had a right to judge them.

D. The Reality of Judgment Deserved

The questions are often asked: "How can man be held responsible for his sin? How can God's wrath be deserved, especially when its recipients have never been told the truth concerning God?" Now listen to me: God never judges unless judgment is deserved. He's a God of absolute justice, and if He judges and pours out wrath, then there is every confidence in my heart that such divine action is exactly what is right and proper in that situation.

The wrath of God is deserved, and we are going to see in Romans 1:19-23 the answers to those two questions. This passage provides us with four reasons for the wrath of God: revelation, rejection, rationalization, and religion.

Lesson

I. REVELATION (vv. 19-20)

"Because that which may be known of God is manifest in them; for God hath shown it unto them. For the invisible things of him from the creation of the world are clearly seen, being understood by the things that are made, even his eternal power and Godhead, so that they are without excuse."

A. Its Communication to All Men

Revelation is one reason God reveals His wrath against men: Men have been given the truth of God regardless of who they are or where they live. If man is "without God" (Eph. 2:12), it is not because God has not revealed Himself to man but because man will not receive God—and therefore God forsakes him.

Although God has revealed Himself to all men, this passage under consideration refers primarily to the Gentiles, because it is dealing with *natural* or *general revelation* (i.e., the revelation of God available to man at large through His creation and sustaining providence). This passage is not talking about the *special revelation* of God through the Scriptures to Israel (Rom. 3:2). Rather, with the Gentile world in view, these verses are indicting man for having suppressed the truth of God that He has revealed entirely apart from special revelation. So all men are "without excuse" (v. 20) and cannot plead ignorance, claiming they have never heard the truth of God because God

34

has made Himself known, and continues to do so, by means of His natural truth in creation. Tertullian, the great early church Father, said, "It was not the pen of Moses that initiated the knowledge of the Creator. The vast majority of mankind, though they had never heard the name of Moses—to say nothing of his book—know the God of Moses nonetheless. Nature is the teacher; the soul is the pupil."

The great story of Helen Keller illustrates the truth that, even without the ability to perceive creation, God can be known by man, "because that which may be known of God is manifest in them" (Rom. 1:19a). As a deaf, mute, and blind girl, Helen Keller had absolutely no capacity to communicate until Anne Sullivan spent endless hours, days, and months to unlock communication. When Anne attempted to tell Helen about God, Helen's response was, "I already know about Him—I just didn't know His name."

Look at this remarkable passage of Scripture: "[Christ] was the true Light, which lighteth every man that cometh into the world" (John 1:9). Does that mean that all men are saved? No. What it does mean is that all men are illumined with the knowledge of God. Christ is the light that is lighting all men. This is precisely how God can pour out His wrath and maintain His love and justice, for God has given everyone in the world an opportunity to know Him—whether it's through observation of what He has made or through an internal awareness of Him.

B. Its Content Concerning God's Nature

If God, then, has made Himself known to all men, what is it that can be known about Him? Obviously, we can't know everything about God, even through special revelation; but what is knowable and apprehendable to the senses of man is revealed to him and can be known by him. God has revealed to man "his eternal power and Godhead" (v. 20b), both as an apprehended perception and as an external reality.

1. His goodness

In Acts 14:15b-17, Paul is speaking to the men of Lystra about "the living God, who made heaven, and earth, and the sea, and all things that are in them; who in times past allowed all nations to walk in their own ways. Nevertheless he left not himself without witness, in that he did good, and gave us rain from heaven, and fruitful seasons, filling our hearts with food and gladness." In other words, the very goodness of life speaks of the goodness of God—the food, rain, seasons, and joy of living, all speak of a beneficient, loving, gracious Creator.

2. His sovereignty

In Acts 17:22-34, Paul is preaching to the philosophers on Mars' Hill in Athens about the identity of the unknown God whom they worship in ignorance. This, by the way, was reflective of their understanding of the true God, though they didn't know His name. So Paul says, "You know He exists, and you already worship Him, so I'm going to tell you who He is. 'God, who made the world and all things in it, seeing that he is Lord of heaven and earth, dwelleth not in temples made with hands, neither is worshiped with men's hands, as though he needed anything, seeing he giveth to all life, and breath, and all things; and hath made of one blood all nations of men to dwell on all the face of the earth, and hath determined the times before appointed, and the bounds of their habitation, that they should seek the Lord, if perhaps they might feel after him, and find him, though he is not far from every one of us; for in him we live, and move, and have our being'" (vv. 24-28a). In other words, the Creator God is not dependent upon His creatures but rather sovereignly controls all things. If men seek Him, as creatures dependent upon Him for life and destiny, they will find Him, for God has manifested Himself in an undeniable way.

3. His eternal power and Godhead

In Romans 1:20 Paul tells again what we can know about God from creation: "For the invisible things of him from the creation of the world are clearly seen, . . . even his eternal power and Godhead" (v. 20). The "invisible things" of God are His attributes, the essence of His nature. Creation, revealing to man that God has eternal power (unfailing omnipotence) and a divine nature (deity), reflects God's manifold attributes of wisdom, love, and goodness. Let's take a closer look at God's creation and see just how wise and powerful God is.

C. Its Clarity in What Is Seen

1. In ancient times

You might ask, "Has God always been clearly revealed?

Don't we have an advantage today with the advent of modern science?" Even without such instruments as the microscope and telescope, men were able to reflect upon the intricacy of design in creation as well as the vastness of the universe. Here are some things that we often take for granted, which were clearly seen by early man:

a) The flowers—their marvelous arrangement and delicacy.

b) The hydrological cycle—water evaporating into clouds, carried over land, and being deposited.

c) Life itself—the mystery of birth and growth of living things.

d) The seas—their constant motion and tidal changes.

e) The heavenly bodies—the beauty and fixed order of stars and moon and the rising and setting of the sun.

In ancient times, men could understand about God's nature from what they observed in their world. The psalmist proclaimed about 1000 years before Christ, "The heavens declare the glory of God, and the firmament showeth his handiwork" (Ps. 19:1). "He who planted the ear, shall he not hear? He who formed the eye, shall he not see?" (Ps. 94:9). Sitting in awe of creation, the psalmist said, "I remember the days of old; I meditate on all thy works; I muse on the work of thy hands" (Ps. 143:5). In the book of Job, one of the oldest books in the Bible, we can find some staggering statements about the creative power of God and the revelation of His nature (cf. 36:24-42:6).

2. In modern times

Many scientists have tried to attribute the creation of the universe to the theoretical process of evolution. They have led most people to believe that chance was the cause of the beginning of the universe rather than a personal and a powerful God. However, science is unable to explain how the initial matter and energy came to exist. Robert Jastrow, an astrophysicist and director of NASA's Goddard Institute for Space Studies, says:

"Now we see how the astronomical evidence supports the biblical view of the origin of the world. . . . The essential elements in the astronomical and biblical accounts of Genesis are the same. Consider the enormousness of the problem. Science has proved that the Universe exploded into being at a certain moment. It asks, What cause produced this effect? Who or what put the matter and energy into the Universe? And science cannot answer these questions. . . .

"For the scientist who has lived by his faith in the power of reason, the story ends like a bad dream. He has scaled the mountains of ignorance; he is about to conquer the highest peak; as he pulls himself over the final rock, he is greeted by a band of theologians who have been there for centuries" (*God and the Astronomers* [New York: Norton, 1978], pp. 14, 114, 116).

In other words, when you scientifically study the evidence and the problems involved in bringing the universe into existence, the ultimate conclusion is that God is responsible for creation. His "eternal power and Godhead" are put on display in the things He has created. To support this, let us take a closer look at some of the Master Designer's creations.

a) Zoology

(1) Migration—Did you know that some birds navigate by the stars when they migrate? Even if those particular birds are raised inside a building where they have never seen the sky, they can still orient themselves toward home when shown an artificial sky representing a place their species has never been.

(2) Aviation—Of the 5 billion birds in America, there are some that fly 500 miles across the Gulf of Mexico. Mallards can fly at 60 miles per hour, eagles at 100 miles per hour, and falcons can dive at 180 miles per hour.

(3) Protection—The bombardier beetle produces chemicals that mix perfectly and at the right moment explode in the face of the enemy, but the explosion never occurs prematurely and never blows up the beetle.

b) Meteorology

It may be surprising to people in a temperate climate to hear that there are on the average of 1,800 storms in operation at any one time and that the energy expended in those storms amounts to the almost inconceivable figure of 1,300,000,000 horsepower. Just one storm alone, depositing a rain of 4 inches over 10,000 square miles, would require the burning of 640,000,000 tons of coal to evaporate enough water for such a rain. To cool again the vapors thus produced and collect them in clouds would take another 800,000,000 horsepower of refrigeration working day and night for 100 days.

The power of God used in supplying the earth with rain is admittedly only an infinitesimal fraction of what His creation power must be. No wonder the psalmist said, "Power belongeth unto God" (Ps. 62:11b); Nahum said, "The Lord is . . . great in power" (1:3a); and Isaiah said, "In the Lord God is everlasting strength" (26:4b).

c) Astronomy

(1) The earth—Our planet is 25,000 miles in circumference and, weighing 6 septillion, 588 sextillion tons, hangs in space. Spinning at 1000 miles per hour with perfect precision so that time is kept to the split second, the earth careens through space around the sun in an orbit of 580 million miles at over 1000 miles per minute.

(2) Comets—The head of a comet may be from 10,000 to 1,000,000 miles long and the tail as long as 100,000,000 miles; it travels at a speed of 350 miles per second. Now, where is the force for all of this?

(3) The sun—If you could convert the energy the sun gives off into horsepower, you would wind up with 500 million, million, billion horsepower, as each second it burns up to 4 million tons of matter.

(4) The Milky Way—If you were to travel across the galaxy in which our solar system is located, at the speed of 186,000 miles per second, it would take you 125,000 years to cross the Milky Way. Yet, it's amazing to think that our galaxy is only one of millions.

Conclusion
As man looks at creation, marveling at its design, the eternal power and divine nature of God are clearly revealed. Because man can know

that God exists from the observation of what God has made, God renders him without excuse, should he claim that he never had an opportunity to know God. Everybody living on the face of this earth has experienced God in His wisdom, power, and generosity. In every moment of man's existence, in his senses, he has perceived Him. For this reason, the general revelation of God's creation is the foundation of all condemnation—because when God judges, He judges justly with equity, because man is without excuse.

Those of you who know the gospel and the name of God's Son, the Lord Jesus Christ, yet have not chosen to worship your Creator, are without excuse even to a greater degree because you have heard the special revelation of God. Without Christ, there is no escape from God's wrath: "How shall we escape, if we neglect so great salvation?" (Heb. 2:3a). "For the wrath of God is revealed . . . against all . . . who hold the truth in unrighteousness" (Rom. 1:18). Only Christ offers that opportunity to escape God's wrath, for He took upon Himself the wrath all men deserve. If you have never committed your life to Christ, won't you open your heart and confess Him as Lord before another moment passes by?

Focusing on the Facts

1. What is religious universalism? What command of Christ does it directly contradict (see p. 30)?
2. Why was the need for laborers to lead people into the kingdom of God of vital concern to Jesus (Matt. 9:37-38; see pp. 30-31)?
3. What have great men of God always understood that motivated them to reach out to those without Christ (see pp. 31-32)?
4. In what spiritual condition is Israel in 1 Samuel 4 (see p. 32)?
5. What history lesson did the Philistines remember that caused them to be afraid (1 Sam. 4:8; see p. 32)?
6. Does having God on your side automatically guarantee victory for everything you do? Use the Israelites as an example (see p. 33).
7. What did the Philistines do to alleviate the divine wrath they were experiencing? By doing so, what did they show that they understood about God (see pp. 33-34)?
8. Why will God never judge unless judgment is deserved (see p. 34)?
9. Why are some men "without God" (Eph. 2:12; see p. 34)?
10. Define the type of revelation that is in view in Romans 1:19-20 (see p. 34).
11. Why are all men "without excuse" (Rom. 1:20; see pp. 34-35)?
12. God has given everyone in the world an opportunity to know

Him, whether it's through_____of what he has made or through an internal_____of Him (see p. 35).

13. In the book of Acts, what attributes of God's nature does Paul say were evident in creation (see pp. 35-36)?

14. What elements of God's nature are "clearly seen" from God's creation, according to Romans 1:20 (see p. 36)?

15. What are some elements of creation that could have been observed by early man, helping him to understand the nature of God? Support your answer with examples from the Psalms (see p. 37).

16. To what have many scientists falsely attributed the creation of the universe? However, what is science incapable of explaining (see p. 37)?

17. Why are those who know the gospel but have not chosen to worship the Creator without excuse to a greater degree (see p. 40)?

Pondering the Principles

1. Knowing that God's judgment will some day come upon all men, we should be motivated to tell people how accepting Christ's sacrificial death on their behalf will allow them to escape God's inevitable wrath. Read some biographies of men and women of God who had a great burden to reach the lost. Their sacrificial, unselfish desires to preach Christ to all men can inspire us to do the same.

2. You may have been raised to believe in the theory of evolution because no other alternative was offered in your schooling. Or maybe you were told that God created the initial matter but used the process of evolution to perfect His original work. Your conclusion on the issue of creation versus evolution can determine whether you believe you are accountable to a personal God. Boost your faith in God in the midst of our technological age by reading some of the excellent material on the scientific evidence for creationism. Familiarize yourself with some of the arguments for creation so that you can intelligently dialogue with those who don't believe in a living and personal Creator.

3. If you were to travel at the speed of light across the galaxy in which our solar system is located, that journey would take you 125,000 years. Realizing that astronomers estimate there are over 1 billion galaxies that can be photographed telescopically and that no scientific or biblical evidence is available for the existence of

life beyond our earth, consider how great God's redeeming love must be for mankind on this planet. For God not to have entirely destroyed this rebellious planet and started over again highlights His great mercy and wisdom in sending His Son as a man to redeem us. Meditate on Psalm 8 as you respond in praise.

4
Reasons for the Wrath of God— Part 2

Outline

Introduction
A. God's Wrath Depicted
   1. In the Old Testament
     a) Psalms
     b) Jeremiah
     c) Nahum
     d) Isaiah
     e) Deuteronomy
   2. In the New Testament
     a) John the Baptist
       (1) Matthew 3:7*b*
       (2) Matthew 3:12*b*
     b) Paul the apostle
       (1) Acts 24:25*a*
       (2) Romans 2:5-6, 8-9*a*, 16
       (3) Ephesians 5:6
     c) The author of Hebrews
       (1) Hebrews 10:26-27
       (2) Hebrews 12:25*b*
     d) John the apostle
       (1) John 3:36*b*
       (2) Revelation 14:10-11*a*; 19:15
     e) Jesus
B. God's Wrath Denied
   1. The corruptions
     a) Soul sleep
     b) Universal salvation
   2. The cautions
   3. The causes

Review
I. Revelation (vv. 19-20)
II. Rejection (v. 21)
   A. The Crime of Rejection
      1. Its irony
      2. Its indictment
      3. Its incongruity
         a) With God's creation
            (1) Psalm 19:1
            (2) Psalm 148
            (3) Revelation 4:11
         b) With God's command
            (1) Psalm 29:2
            (2) 1 Corinthians 10:31b
   B. The Chronicles of Rejection
      1. In the past
         a) The glory in the Garden
            (1) Revealed
            (2) Rejected
         b) The glory in the wilderness
            (1) Revealed
            (2) Rejected
         c) The glory in the Temple
            (1) Revealed
            (2) Rejected
               (a) Idol worship
               (b) Creature worship
               (c) Tammuz worship
               (d) Sun worship
         d) The glory in the Son
            (1) Revealed
            (2) Rejected
      2. In the future
      3. In the present
   C. The Consequences of Rejection
      1. Thanklessness
      2. Emptiness

Introduction

The apostle Paul began his message of the gospel of Christ by establishing the fact that God is a God of wrath: "for the wrath of God is revealed from heaven" (Rom. 1:18a). Paul realized men need to understand that God is exceedingly angry with them. Men must be confronted with the reality that they stand in inevitable judgment before a holy God who must react to their sin. It is sad that through the years Christians have soft-pedaled the theme of judgment. Hell has been quietly omitted from our preaching; wrath has often been depersonalized, as if God were just an unconcerned, deistic machine. But God is involved in His wrath as much as He is in His grace, mercy, or love. This is made clear in many Scriptures that paint an absolutely fearful and horrifying picture of God's wrath.

A. God's Wrath Depicted

   1. In the Old Testament

      a) Psalms

         (1) Psalm 58:10—"The righteous will rejoice when he sees the vengeance; he shall wash his feet in the blood of the wicked."

         (2) Psalm 68:21*a*—"But God shall wound the head of his enemies."

         (3) Psalm 69:27—"Add to them punishment upon punishment; may they have no acquittal from Thee" (RSV*).

         (4) Psalm 79:12—"Return sevenfold into the bosom of our neighbors the taunts with which they have taunted Thee, O Lord!" (RSV).

         (5) Psalm 109:12—"Let there be none to extend kindness to him, nor any to pity his fatherless children!" (RSV).

         (6) Psalm 137:9—"Happy shall he be that taketh and dasheth thy little ones against the stones."

         (7) Psalm 139:21-22—"Do not I hate them, that hate thee O Lord? And am not I grieved with those who rise up against thee? I hate them with perfect hatred; I count them mine enemies."

Some people are so unable to deal with the wrath of God as revealed in the Psalms, that they just exclude them from the Christian Scriptures altogether. In the London newspaper *The Times* ("Psalms Chosen from New Testament" [23 August 1962]), there was an article that said that earlier in that year fourteen church study groups in Woodford, Essex, looked at the Old Testament psalms and concluded that eighty-four of them were "not fit for

* Revised Standard Version.

Christians to sing." In commenting about those eighty-four psalms, the Reverend Christopher Wansey, rector of a church in Woodford, said, "These psalms and parts of many others are full of tribal jealousies, bloodthirsty threats and curses, whinings and moanings, which are shocking in themselves and timewasting to God and man. The New Testament psalms are Christian through and through."

b) Jeremiah

After many prayers of intercession for the benefit of Judah, Jeremiah came to the place where he finally understood God's wrath:

(1) Jeremiah 18:19-21, 23*b*—"Give heed to me, O Lord, and hearken to my plea. Is evil a recompense for good? Yet they have dug a pit for my life. Remember how I stood before Thee to speak good for them, to turn away Thy wrath from them. Therefore deliver up their children to famine; give them over to the power of the sword, let their wives become childless and widowed. May their men meet death by pestilence, their youths be slain by the sword in battle. Forgive not their iniquity, nor blot out sin from Thy sight" (RSV).

Did Jeremiah accurately reflect the true nature of God's wrath? Here is God's response to Jeremiah's plea:

(2) Jeremiah 19:3*b*-9*a*—"Behold, I am bringing such evil upon this place that the ears of every one who hears of it will tingle . . . because they have filled this place with the blood of innocents, and have built the high place of Baal to burn their sons in the fire as burnt offerings to Baal, . . . therefore, behold, days are coming, says the Lord, when this place shall no more be called Topheth, or the valley of the son of Hinnom, but the valley of Slaughter. . . . I will give their dead bodies for food to the birds of the air and to the beasts of the earth. And I will make this city a horror, a thing to be hissed at; every one who passes by it will be horrified and will hiss because of all its disasters. And I will make them eat the flesh of their sons and their daughters . . . " (RSV).

46

c) Nahum

"The Lord is a jealous God and avenging, the Lord is avenging and wrathful; the Lord takes vengeance on His adversaries and keeps wrath for His enemies. The Lord is slow to anger and of great might, and the Lord will by no means clear the guilty. . . . Who can stand before His indignation? Who can endure the heat of His anger? His wrath is poured out like fire, and rocks are broken asunder by Him. . . . Woe to the bloody city . . . " (1:2-3*a*, 6; 3:1*a*, RSV).

d) Isaiah

"Behold, the day of the Lord comes, cruel, with wrath and fierce anger, to make the earth a desolation and to destroy its sinners from it. Their infants will be dashed in pieces before their eyes; their houses will be plundered and their wives ravished" (13:9, 16 RSV).

e) Deuteronomy

Moses gave direction that, upon entry into the Promised Land, the Israelites were to invoke God's curse upon such of their number as did not obey God's commandments. In chapters 27-28 there are recorded in more than fifty verses detailed judgments for those who violate God's commandments.

Now we realize that those fearful verses of judgment are the authoritative statements of God's truth in His Word. The God of the Old Testament is clearly a God of wrath, and though some people assume that such a picture is not represented in the New Testament, they are obviously not in agreement with what the Bible reveals there.

2. In the New Testament

a) John the Baptist

(1) Matthew 3:7*b*—"You brood of vipers, who warned you to flee from the wrath to come?" (NASB).

(2) Matthew 3:12*b*—"He [Christ] will gather His wheat into the barn, but He will burn up the chaff with unquenchable fire" (NASB).

47

b) Paul the apostle

(1) Acts 24:25*a*—"And as he [Paul] reasoned of righteousness, self-control, and judgment to come, Felix trembled."

(2) Romans 2:5-6, 8-9*a*, 16—"But by your hard and impenitent heart you are storing up wrath for yourself on the day of wrath when God's righteous judgment will be revealed. For He will render to every man according to his works. . . . for those who are factious and do not obey the truth, but obey wickedness, there will be wrath and fury. There will be tribulation and distress for every human being who does evil. . . . on that day when, according to my gospel, God judges the secrets of men by Christ Jesus" (RSV).

(3) Ephesians 5:6—"Let no one deceive you with empty words, for it is because of these things that the wrath of God comes upon the sons of disobedience" (RSV).

c) The author of Hebrews

(1) Hebrews 10:26-27—"For if we sin deliberately after receiving the knowledge of the truth, there no longer remains a sacrifice for sins, but a fearful prospect of judgment, and a fury of fire which will consume the adversaries" (RSV).

(2) Hebrews 12:25*b*—"For if they did not escape when they refused him who warned them on earth, much less shall we escape if we reject Him who warns from heaven" (RSV).

d) John the apostle

(1) John 3:36*b*—"He who does not obey the Son shall not see life, but the wrath of God rests upon Him" (RSV).

(2) Revelation 14:10-11*a*; 19:15 —"He also shall drink the wine of God's wrath, poured unmixed into the cup of His anger, and he shall be tormented with fire and brimstone in the presence of the holy angels and in the presence of the Lamb. And the smoke of their torment goes up for ever and ever; and they have no rest, day or night. . . . From His mouth issues a sharp sword with which

to smite the nations, and He will rule them with a rod of iron; He will tread the wine press of the fury of the wrath of God the Almighty" (RSV).

    e) Jesus

Though our Lord was filled with compassion and concern, He nevertheless spoke frequently of judgment (Matt. 10:15), perdition (Matt. 16:26), hell (Matt. 5:29-30), eternal punishment (Matt. 18:6-8), and other aspects of the grim reality of God's wrath.

The entire Bible is supportive of the truth that God is a God of wrath. However, many are denying this today. In an attempt to escape accountability to a holy God, many deny God's wrath.

B. God's Wrath Denied

    1. The corruptions

        a) Soul sleep—The first denial comes in the form of a doctrine that teaches that when you die, if you are condemned, you just go into an eternal sleep and never suffer anything (cf. Mark 9:42-48; Luke 16:19-31).

        b) Universal salvation—The second denial is the doctrine that teaches that everyone will be saved.

    2. The cautions

        a) Beware of the powerful, natural appeal of universalism and soul sleep—they ignore the reality of eternal torment.

        b) Beware of the pervasive influence of theological liberalism—it distorts the character of Christ.

        c) Beware that such doctrines are cultic—they are not in agreement with the Bible.

        d) Beware of the denial of the existence of hell—it will result in the loss of zeal for winning souls because the motivation for speaking God's truth will be drastically crippled.

    3. The causes

R. A. Torrey provides for us the causes of, and solutions to, such erroneous views: "Shallow views of sin and of God's holiness, and of the glory of Jesus Christ and His claims upon us, lie at the bottom of weak theories of the doom of the impenitent. When we see sin in all its hideousness and enormity, the Holiness of God in all its

49

perfection, and the glory of Jesus Christ in all its infinity, nothing but a doctrine that those who persist in the choice of sin, who love darkness rather than light, and who persist in the rejection of the Son of God, shall endure everlasting anguish, will satisfy the demands of our own moral intuitions. . . . the more closely men walk with God and the more devoted they become to His service, the more likely they are to believe this doctrine" (*What the Bible Teaches* [New York: Revell, 1898], pp. 311-13).

Review

Now that brings us to the question that is answered in verses 19 through 23: If God is going to judge, is He fair in doing so? In our last lesson, we saw that God is justified in condemning man.

I. REVELATION (vv. 19-20; see pp. 34-40)

Creation has provided man with enough light for him to perceive God's sustaining power and deity. But unfortunately, man has rejected the truth and turned further away from God; for had he accepted the truth of God visible in creation, God would have given more light of divine revelation to him. If a man goes to hell, he goes there because he has openly and personally chosen to reject the revelation of God. Even if he had never heard the gospel, God would have revealed the whole message of redemption to him if he had lived up to the light of God's initial revelation.

II. REJECTION (v. 21)

"Because, when they knew God, they glorified him not as God, neither were thankful, but became vain in their imaginations, and their foolish heart was darkened."

Whereas *revelation* has shown us that God has revealed Himself to men, *rejection* informs us that men have turned away from that revelation. This becomes the second reason for God's condemning men.

Man has rejected the revelation of God in creation—the very thing that was designed to lead him to God. Surely, man has committed a very serious crime.

A. The Crime of Rejection

  1. Its irony

    Donald Grey Barnhouse has written a potent statement in this regard: "Will God give man brains to see these things and will man then fail to exercise his will toward that God? The sorrowful answer is that both of these things are true. God will give a man brains to smelt iron and make a hammer head and nails. God will grow a tree and give man strength to cut it down and brains to fashion a hammer handle from its wood. And when man has the hammer and the nails, God will put out His hand and let man drive nails through it and place Him on a cross in the supreme demonstration that men are without excuse" (*Romans*, vol. 1 [Grand Rapids: Eerdmans, 1953], p. 245).

In other words, it is ironic that the things God gave man to lead him to Himself became the very things man used to crucify Christ. Rather than acting in accord with the truth, men actively oppose it.

2. Its indictment

Exactly what charges are brought against this crime of rejecting God? "Because, when they knew God, they glorified him not as God" (v. 21*a*). The worst crime ever committed in the universe is the failure to give God glory. This is the very essence of the fallenness of man—he refuses to glorify God. When man will not recognize the divine attributes of God and that He alone is worthy of exaltation, honor, adoration, and praise—man has committed the ultimate affrontery to God. The very reason man has been created is to glorify the One to whom glory is due (cf. Lev. 10:3; 1 Chron. 16:24-29; Ps. 148; Isa. 48:1-11; Rom. 15:5-6).

What Is the glory of God?

The glory of God is the summation of all of God's attributes, which constitute His entire being. God has revealed to man different elements of His glory:

1. Power—"Christ was raised up from the dead by the glory of the Father" (Rom. 6:4*b*).

2. Goodness—"And he [Moses] said, I beseech thee, show me thy glory. And he [God] said, I will make all my goodness pass before thee" (Ex. 33:18-19*a*). His goodness is His attributes, such as grace and mercy.

3. Grace and truth—"And the Word [God the Son] was made flesh, and dwelt among us (and we beheld his glory, the glory as of the only begotten of the Father), full of grace and truth" (John 1:14).

But glorifying God is precisely what men by nature will not do: "For all have sinned, and come short of the glory of God" (Rom. 3:23). They refuse to see His glorious attributes and consequently will not manifest that glory in their own lives.

3. Its incongruity

a) With God's creation

Did you know that the rest of God's created world is designed to give God glory?

(1) Psalm 19:1—"The heavens declare the glory of God, and the firmament showeth his handiwork."

(2) Psalm 148—All God's creation is invoked to "praise . . . the Lord."

(3) Revelation 4:11—"Thou art worthy, O Lord, to receive glory and honor and power; for thou hast created all things, and for thy pleasure they are and were created."

And as we saw in our previous lesson, all of God's creation glorifies Him by manifesting His mighty handiwork.

b) With God's command

But in the midst of all of God's creation, man defiantly refuses to recognize and glorify God—even though he too is designed for this purpose:

(1) Psalm 29:2—"Give unto the Lord the glory due unto his name; worship the Lord in the beauty of holiness" (cf. Ps. 148:12-13).

(2) 1 Corinthians 10:31b—"Whatever ye do, do all to the glory of God."

He who can stand in the midst of this created universe and look around in our day and time and yet say that he does not believe in God is the biggest fool who ever lived. With all the evidence of creation around us, let us not be guilty of failing to glorify our Creator.

B. The Chronicles of Rejection

God has always desired that man would see His glory. God created man to have fellowship with Him, yet when the glory of God has been repeatedly revealed to him throughout history, man has consistently shunned God's offer to know, to love, and to serve Him.

1. In the past

   a) The glory in the Garden

      (1) Revealed—Genesis 2

      God manifested His presence to Adam and Eve. At first, they recognized and accepted God's glory as they communed with Him, but then they sinned in rebellion against God's command.

      (2) Rejected—Genesis 3

      "And they heard the voice of the Lord God walking [anthropomorphic movement of the *Shekinah*—God's glory] in the garden in the cool of the day: and Adam and his wife hid themselves from the presence of the Lord God among the trees of the garden" (3:8). God had said, "Obey Me, and do not eat of the tree of the knowledge of good and evil—that's what I ask of you. Glorify Me by your obedience to My command." But, deceitfully tempted by Satan to disobey and eat and thereby become "as God" (3:5), Adam and Eve disregarded God's command, seeking their own glory. That's exactly what Romans 1:21a is saying: "Because when they knew God, they glorified him not as God."

      Would you say Adam has an excuse if he were to be condemned? Not at all! He knew what it was to perceive and know God, and he could have obeyed. Adam was expelled from the Garden, having made his choice to turn his back on the knowledge of God.

   Now God could have chosen to start over from scratch at that point and recreate a new human race. But God desired to seek out fallen, sinful man and draw him back into a relationship with Him. So God endeavored again to reveal His glory.

   b) The glory in the wilderness

   Next, God chose to reveal His glory in the nation of Israel, whom He designed for this special purpose (cf. Ex. 19:4-6; Deut. 7:6-11; Isa. 43:7; 44:23).

(1) Revealed—Exodus 33-34

At this point in Israel's history, God had brought the nation out of Egypt with His great power under the leadership of Moses. Overwhelmed with the apparent impossibility of the task before him, Moses requested of God that He provide some form of tangible, physical encouragement for him and that He show him His glory (33:12-18). Having agreed to allow His presence to go with Moses and to show him His glory, God said, "I will make all my goodness pass before thee and I will proclaim the name of the Lord before thee, and will be gracious to whom I will be gracious, and will show mercy on whom I will show mercy" (33:19; cf. 34:5-7). In other words, God said, "I will let you see My glory by showing you My name (i.e., attributes) which is good, merciful, gracious, long-suffering, truthful, forgiving, and just."

(2) Rejected—Exodus, Numbers

Though it was clear that God had revealed Himself to Israel and in a personal way to Moses, unto whom the Lord spoke "face to face, as a man speaketh unto his friend" (Ex. 33:11), Israel still refused to give God the glory He deserved. In spite of God's deliverance from Egypt and His visual presence and sustaining providence in the wilderness, the nation of Israel complained and rebelled against God and His chosen leader, Moses. Indicting their rebellious spirit, Moses said, "You have rejected the Lord who is among you and have wept before Him, saying, 'Why did we ever leave Egypt?' " (Num. 11:20b, NASB; cf. Ps. 78).

How much more prominent could God have made His presence to Israel than to lead them during the day by a cloud and during the night by a pillar of fire; and even to dwell among them as His glory filled the Tabernacle (Ex. 40:34-38)? Yet, in spite of God's revelation, Israel refused to respond in faith to the glory of God. And as a result, that disobedient and unbelieving generation died in the wilderness without entering the Promised Land (Heb. 3:8-11, 16-19).

God patiently chose to continue to manifest His glory in Israel. But the movable Tabernacle was superceded by the building of the Solomonic Temple in Jerusalem.

c) The glory in the Temple

   (1) Revealed—1 Kings 8

   "And it came to pass, when the priests were come out of the holy place, that the cloud filled the house of the Lord, so that the priests could not stand to minister because of the cloud; for the glory of the Lord had filled the house of the Lord" (8:10-11). And at his dedicatory sermon, Solomon said, "I have surely built thee an house to dwell in, a settled place for thee to abide in forever" (8:13). But was Solomon right? Did the Temple remain a place that God's glory would "abide in forever"? No, because Israel refused to see the glory—they turned their back on it just as men always have.

   (2) Rejected—Ezekiel 8

   God showed to the prophet Ezekiel a vision of the desecrations that were taking place in the Jerusalem Temple. He wanted the new generation, born and growing up in captivity in Babylon, to see His righteousness in the present chastening.

   (a) Idol worship (vv. 4-6; cf. Lev. 26:1)

   "And, behold, the glory of the God of Israel was there, according to the vision that I [Ezekiel] saw in the plain. Then said he unto me, Son of man, lift up thine eyes now in the way toward the north. So I lifted up mine eyes in the way toward the north, and, behold, northward at the gate of the altar this image of jealousy in the entrance. [There's an idol in the entrance to the temple.] He said furthermore unto me, Son of man, seest thou what they do? Even the great abominations that the house of Israel committeth here, that I should go far off from my sanctuary? But turn yet again, and thou shalt see greater abominations."

(b) Creature worship (vv. 7-12)

"And he brought me to the door of the court; and when I looked, behold, a hole in the wall. [In other words, The Temple is in disarray—they aren't even taking care of it.] Then said he unto me, Son of man, dig now in the wall; and when I had digged in the wall, behold, a door. And he said unto me, Go in, and behold the wicked abominations that they do here. So I went in and saw; and, behold, every form of creeping things, and abominable beasts, and all the idols of the house of Israel, portrayed upon the wall round about. And there stood before them seventy men of the ancients of the house of Israel, and in the midst of them stood Jaazaniah, the son of Shaphan, with every man his censer in his hand; and a thick cloud of incense went up. Then said he unto me, Son of man, hast thou seen what the ancients of the house of Israel do in the dark, every man in the chambers of his imagery? For they say, The Lord seeth us not; the Lord hath forsaken the earth."

(c) Tammuz worship (vv. 13-14)

"He said also unto me, Turn yet again, and thou shalt see greater abominations that they do. Then he brought me to the door of the gate of the Lord's house, which was toward the north; and, behold, there sat women weeping for Tammuz [another name for Baal]."

(d) Sun worship (vv. 15-16)

"Then said he unto me, Hast thou seen this, O Son of man? Turn yet again, and thou shalt see greater abominations than these. And he brought me into the inner court of the Lord's house, and, behold, at the door of the temple of the Lord, between the porch and the altar, were about five and twenty men, with their backs toward the temple of the Lord, and their faces toward the east; and they worshiped the sun toward the east.

"Then he said unto me, Hast thou seen this, O Son of man? Is it a light thing to the house of Judah that they commit the abominations which they commit here? For they have filled the land with violence, and have returned to provoke me to anger; and, lo, they put the branch to their nose. Therefore will I also deal in fury; mine eye shall not spare, neither will I have pity; and though they cry in mine ears with a loud voice, yet will I not hear them" (vv. 17-18).

In refusing to glorify God, the people of Israel so desecrated the Temple in which God had chosen to manifest His glory that God removed His presence from them (in sequence, Ezek. 9:3; 10:4, 18; 11:23). This departure of the divine glory marked the end of the theocratic kingdom in Old Testament history. But was this to be the last time God would manifest His glory?

d) The glory in the Son

(1) Revealed—John 1

"And the Word was made flesh, and dwelt among us (and we beheld his glory, the glory as of the only begotten of the Father), full of grace and truth" (1:14). The Greek word for "dwelt" means "tabernacled." The glory of God revealed in the Old Testament Tabernacle was now revealed in the New Testament in the tabernacle of God's Son. In fact, three of the disciples were allowed to see the shining brilliance of God's glory in the transfiguration of Christ on the mountain (Luke 9:27-36; cf. 2 Pet. 1:15-18). He was the glory of God—the same glory that walked and talked in the Garden, the same glory that shone on the face of Moses, the same glory that dwelt in the Tabernacle, the same glory that departed from the Temple—that same glory came in a human tabernacle.

Though God, in Christ, demonstrated His love, mercy, goodness, power, wisdom, grace, truth, and the other divine attributes, did men desire to reflect that glory of God in their own lives?

57

(2) Rejected—John 1

"He was in the world, and the world was made by him, and the world knew him not. He came unto his own, and his own received him not" (1:10-11). There were some who received Him; throughout history there's always been the faithful remnant that has glorified God—but the majority rejected Him and shouted, "Away with Him . . . crucify him. . . . We have no king but Caesar" (John 19:15; cf. Matt. 21:33-46; Luke 19:11-27).

The whole history of Scripture is the history of God revealing His glory. But you ask, "What about the future? Will God's glory come again?"

2. In the future

"Immediately after the tribulation of those days shall the sun be darkened, and the moon shall not give its light, and the stars shall fall from heaven, and the powers of the heavens shall be shaken. And then shall appear the sign of the Son of man in heaven; and then shall all the tribes of the earth mourn, and they shall see the Son of man coming in the clouds of heaven with power and great glory" (Matt. 24:29-30). You see, all the lights will go out, and then will come the blazing *Shekinah* revelation of the glory of God which will fill God's kingdom with light (Isa. 60:1-3, 19-21; Rev. 22:5).

Well, we've seen that God has filled the past and the future with the revelation of His glory, but what about the present?

3. In the present

God is revealing His glory in the world today. Do you want to know how? Look at Colossians 1:27: "Christ in you, the hope of glory." God's whole plan of redemption in the church, the Body of Christ, is to constantly be revealing His glory (Eph. 1). We are the radiation of Christ's glory in the world today, and men don't listen to us any more than they did to Christ. Man always refuses God's glory.

C. The Consequences of Rejection

1. Thanklessness

"Because, when they knew God, they glorified him not as God, neither were thankful" (v. 21a). In other words, men are so *prideful* that they can't be *thankful*. They refuse to ascribe everything they possess to the God who, out of His goodness, gave it graciously to them (cf. James 1:17; Matt. 5:45). Man's biggest failure is not that he fails to recognize God, but that he refuses to glorify God. And if he does not accept God as the source of everything, he will not thank Him—and not to thank God is blasphemous.

2. Emptiness

Instead of glorifying God and having thankful hearts, men "became vain in their imaginations, and their foolish heart was darkened" (Rom. 1:21b). In other words, when men reject the revelation of God, their thoughts and self-willed reasonings become empty and purposeless. As a result, into that spiritual vacuum comes the darkness of blindness and unrighteousness that floods their foolish hearts.

If men reject the truth God has revealed, they become blindly unable to find it. That's why Jesus said to those who had rejected Him as their Messiah, "And because I tell you the truth, ye believe me not" (John 8:45; cf. 8:47; 9:39-41). That's also why Paul said, "But the natural man receiveth not the things of the Spirit of God; for they are foolishness unto him, neither can he know them, because they are spiritually discerned" (1 Cor. 2:14). Without the "mind of Christ" (1 Cor. 2:16), man's mind is filled with senseless, empty, evil thoughts. This is the legacy of man's refusal to glorify God. And it's not just intellectual darkness, but moral darkness as well.

Truly, this passage in Romans is a tragic commentary on man's unrelenting rejection of God's revelation. "Professing themselves to be wise, they became fools" (Rom. 1:22).

Focusing on the Facts

1. What reality must all men be confronted with (see p. 44)?
2. What difference between the Old and New Testaments do some people see with regard to God's wrath (see pp. 45-46)?
3. Name some New Testament characters who clearly spoke of God's wrath (see pp. 47-49).
4. Explain two doctrines that deny that God's wrath will ever be experienced after this life (see p. 49).

5. If you deny the existence of hell, what will happen as a result? Why (see p. 49)?
6. What lie "at the bottom of weak theories of the doom of the impenitent," according to R. A. Torrey (see p. 49)?
7. What is "the supreme demonstration that men are without excuse," according to Donald Grey Barnhouse (see p. 51)?
8. Rather than acting in accord with the truth, what do many men do instead (see p. 51)?
9. What is the worst crime ever committed against God (see p. 51)?
10. Why was man created? Support your answer with Scripture (see p. 51).
11. What is the glory of God (see pp. 52-53)?
12. How is man's failure to glorify God incongruous with the rest of creation (see p. 52)?
13. Whose glory did Adam and Eve seek in Genesis 3 (see p. 53)?
14. In spite of God's delivering the Israelites from Egypt and sustaining them the wilderness, how did the nation manifest its rejection of God? What was the consequence of Israel's refusal to glorify God (see pp. 54-55)?
15. What did the Lord reveal to Ezekiel about the nature of Israel's worship that led to their captivity in Babylon (see pp. 55-57)?
16. What marked the end of the theocratic kingdom in the Old Testament (see p. 57)?
17. Explain how God's glory was revealed and later rejected, according to John 1 (see pp. 57-58).
18. How is God revealing His glory in the world today (see pp. 58-59)?
19. If man does not accept God as the source of everything, what will he fail to do as a result (Rom. 1:21; see p. 59)?
20. What fills the spiritual vacuum of those who reject the revelation of God (see p. 59) ?

Pondering the Principles

1. A shallow view of sin, God's holiness, Christ's deity, and God's claims upon His creatures will lead people to deny that God will judge those who reject His grace. Do you have a solid understanding of each of those areas? If you are to effectively help people in our society accept God's gracious provision for salvation, they need to know that all men have sinned and are accountable to a holy God. That may not be a pleasant message for someone who denies the existence of a personal God or who believes that God is so loving that He would never judge anyone, but it is an important one. Find at least two verses for each of the

four areas mentioned and be ready to explain them to unbelievers as opportunities arise.

2. Romans 1:21 says that a man who has rejected God's truth does not give Him thanks. But thankfulness to God is to be a constant part of the Christian life. Look up the following verses to learn what the Bible says about thankfulness: Philippians 4:6; Colossians 3:15-17; 1 Thessalonians 5:18; 1 Timothy 2:1; and Hebrews 13:15. The next time you gather as a family or as a group of believers, make an opportunity for everyone present to offer thanks to God for at least one thing in his life.

5
Reasons for the Wrath of God—
Part 3

Outline

Introduction
A. Prophecies of Judgment
B. Parables of Judgment

Review
 I. Revelation (vv. 19-20)
 II. Rejection (v. 21)
    A. Contrasted
    B. Characterized
       1. The refusal to glorify God
       2. The results of not glorifying God
          a) Darkness
             (1) Intellectual
             (2) Moral
          b) Deception
 III. Rationalization (v. 22)
     A. Compromise
        1. Theistic evolution
        2. Liberal theology
        3. Psychology
     B. Confrontation

Introduction

Paul began the message of the good news of Jesus Christ with the reality of "the wrath of God" which "is revealed . . . against all ungodliness" (Rom. 1:18a). If you think it is unusual that this great epistle on the doctrine of salvation opens with this statement about judgment, maybe it's because you are not aware that the New Testament opens this way in the gospel of Matthew (cf. Matt. 3:1-12; 4:17). Paul is only following the example of our Lord, who had more to say about judgment, destruction, damnation, and hell, than anybody else recorded in Scripture.

A. Prophecies of Judgment

1. For contempt of others (Matt. 5:22)

   "But I say unto you that whosoever is angry with his brother without a cause shall be in danger of judgment; and whosoever shall say to his brother, Raca, shall be in danger of the council; but whosoever shall say, Thou fool, shall be in danger of hell fire."

2. For unwillingness to forsake sin (Matt. 5:29-30)

   "And if thy right eye offend thee, pluck it out, and cast it from thee; for it is profitable for thee that one of thy members should perish, and not that thy whole body should be cast into hell. And if thy right hand offend thee, cut it off, and cast it from thee; for it is profitable for thee that one of thy members should perish, and not that thy whole body should be cast into hell."

3. For falsely professing to follow Christ (Matt. 7:22-23)

   "Many will say to me in that day, Lord, Lord, have we not prophesied in they name? And in thy name have cast out demons? And in thy name done many wonderful works? And then will I profess unto them, I never knew you; depart from me, ye that work iniquity."

4. For assuming Jewish lineage can save (Matt. 8:12)

   "But the sons of the kingdom shall be cast out into outer darkness; there shall be weeping and gnashing of teeth."

5. For rejecting the messengers of Christ (Matt. 10:15)

   "Verily I say unto you, It shall be more tolerable for the land of Sodom and Gomorrah in the day of judgment, than for that city."

6. For failing to fear and reverence God (Matt. 10:28)

   "And fear not them who kill the body, but are not able to kill the soul; but rather fear him who is able to destroy both soul and body in hell."

7. For speaking careless words (Matt. 12:36)

   "But I say unto you that every idle word that men shall speak, they shall give account of it in the day of judgment."

8. For refusing to repent after having greater revelation (Matt. 12:41)

"The men of Nineveh shall rise in judgment with this generation, and shall condemn it; because they repented at the preaching of Jonah; and, behold, a greater than Jonah is here."

B. Parables of Judgment

1. For falsely professing to follow Christ (Matt. 13:40-42; cf. 13:49)

"As, therefore, the tares are gathered and burned in the fire, so shall it be in the end of this age. The Son of man shall send forth his angels, and they shall gather out of his kingdom all things that offend, and them who do iniquity, and shall cast them into a furnace of fire; there shall be wailing and gnashing of teeth."

2. For selfishly loving the world system (Matt. 16:26; cf. Luke 16:19-31)

"For what is a man profited, if he shall gain the whole world, and lose his own soul? Or what shall a man give in exchange for his soul?"

3. For refusing to forgive (Matt. 18:34-35)

"And his lord was angry, and delivered him to the inquisitors [torturers], till he should pay all that was due unto him. So likewise shall my heavenly Father do also unto you, if ye, from your hearts, forgive not every one his brother his trespasses."

4. For shamefully treating and slaying God's messengers (Matt. 22:7; cf. 21:33-46; 23:33-36)

"But when the king heard of it, he was angry; and he sent forth his armies, and destroyed those murderers, and burned up their city."

5. For hypocritically serving God (Matt. 24:50-51)

"The lord of that servant shall come in a day when he looketh not for him, and in an hour that he is not aware of, and shall cut him asunder, and appoint him his portion with the hypocrites; there shall be weeping and gnashing of teeth."

6. For unfaithful stewardship (Matt. 25:26-28a, 30)

"His lord answered and said unto him, Thou wicked and slothful servant, thou knewest that I reap where I sowed not, and gather where I have not spread? Thou oughtest, therefore, to have put my money to the exchangers, and then, at my coming, I should have received mine own with interest. Take, therefore, the talent from him. . . . And cast the unprofitable servant into outer darkness; there shall be weeping and gnashing of teeth."

So, do you see the point I am trying to make? From the testimony of our Lord Himself, it is clear from the very beginning that God is a God of judgment and wrath, who punishes sin. Therefore, we are not surprised, as we approach the epistle to the Romans, to find the apostle Paul beginning his gospel presentation with a statement warning men about the wrath of God. Following that statement in verse 18, Paul answers the criticism that God is unfair, overbearing, and even unloving, by defending God's right to respond in judgment. To vindicate God's judgment and to chronicle the decline and fall of man, Paul sets forth four reasons for God's wrath, the first being *revelation*.

Review

I. REVELATION (vv. 19-20; see pp. 34-40, 50)

The first reason God can righteously act in judgment against man is that men have been given the truth of God—God has disclosed Himself, in His created order, to everyone. Therefore, man is responsible for responding appropriately to the revelation of God's truth.

As believers we are responsible for bringing that revelation to men, preaching "the gospel to every creature" (Mark 16:15; cf. Matt. 28:19, Luke 24:47); for without the special revelational knowledge of Christ, there is no salvation. No one is ever saved short of faith in Jesus Christ, now that He has paid the price on the cross for every sin committed in the past or to be committed in the future.

Now this may seem like an impossible task, but I really believe that God, in His sovereignty and justice, will somehow bring the knowledge of Christ to those whom He has chosen for salvation, as they live up to the light they have already received. Just remember, God always responds to a seeking heart: "Ye shall seek me, and find me, when ye shall search for me with all your heart" (Jer. 29:13; cf. Deut. 4:29; 1 Chron. 28:9b; Ps. 145:18; John

7:17; Heb. 11:6). Jesus said it this way: "All that the Father giveth me shall come to me; and him that cometh to me I will in no wise cast out" (John 6:37).

II. REJECTION (v. 21; see pp. 50-59)

After having revealed His nature to man in creation, *God is rejected by man, who has refused to thank and glorify Him*. Throughout history, God has manifested His glorious presence in various ways, yet man's response has always been the same: Whether it was the glory of the Shekinah presence in the garden or the glory in the Son, man has failed to glorify God and sought rather to glorify himself.

We have already looked briefly into the concept of glorifying God, but it is so utterly important that I feel it is necessary to expand our understanding of what it means to glorify God. If we understand what that means, then we can also understand what not glorifying God consists of.

A. Contrasted

What are some practical ways in which we can glorify God?

1. By confessing Jesus as Lord

   "Every tongue should confess that Jesus Christ is Lord, to the *glory* of God, the Father" (Phil. 2:11, italics added).

2. By making it our goal to glorify Him

   "Whether, therefore, ye eat, or drink, or whatever ye do, do all to the *glory* of God" (1 Cor. 10:31, italics added). Even the most ordinary activities of life should be done in a way that honors God.

3. By confessing our sin

   "And Joshua said unto Achan, My son, give, I pray thee, *glory* to the Lord God of Israel, and make confession unto him, and tell me now what thou hast done; hide it not from me" (Josh. 7:19, italics added). When we sin, God reacts in a holy manner by chastening us; and as we admit our sin, we affirm the fact that we deserve the chastening and thereby uphold God's justice and holiness.

4. By trusting in Him

   "He [Abraham] staggered not at the promise of God through unbelief, but was strong in faith, giving *glory* to God" (Rom. 4:20, italics added). When you believe what

God has said, you uphold His faithfulness and trust-worthiness.

Keep in mind that these ways of glorifying God are the very things unbelieving man refuses to do. The unbelieving world obviously does not acknowledge the lordship of Christ, nor do they live their lives for God's glory. They deny that they have sinned (1 John 1:8, 10), for they do not believe the Scriptures and the God revealed in them. Unbelieving men will not trust God for their destiny. They simply and tragically refuse to glorify Him. Let's continue to look at some other ways believers *can* glorify God and, conversely, ways in which unbelievers *fail* to glorify Him.

5. By praising Him

"Whoso offereth praise *glorifieth* me" (Ps. 50:23*a*, italics added). We praise God by honoring Him for who He is and what He has done (cf. Ps. 145).

6. By praying

"And whatever ye shall ask in my name, that will I do, that the Father may be *glorified* in the Son" (John 14:13, italics added). Prayer gives God an opportunity to be glorified as we see His power and love in action.

7. By ministering our gifts

"As every man hath received the gift, even so minister the same one to another, as good stewards of the manifold grace of God. If any man speak, let him speak as the oracles of God; if any man minister, let him do it as of the ability which God giveth, that God in all things may be *glorified* through Jesus Christ, to whom be praise and dominion forever and ever. Amen" (1 Pet. 4:10-11, italics added).

8. By proclaiming the Word

"Finally, brethren, pray for us, that the word of the Lord may have free course, and be *glorified*, even as it is with you" (2 Thess. 3:1, italics added; cf. 1 Thess. 1:8).

9. By moral purity

"Flee fornication. Every sin that a man doeth is outside the body; but he that committeth fornication sinneth against his own body. What? Know ye not that your body is the temple of the Holy Spirit who is in you, whom ye have of God, and ye are not your own? For ye are bought with a price; therefore, *glorify* God in your body and in your spirit, which are God's" (1 Cor. 6:18-20, italics added).

10. By winning people to Jesus Christ

"That the abundant grace might through the thanksgiving of many redound to the *glory* of God" (2 Cor. 4:15b, italics added). When people are saved, God is glorified because His grace is being manifested, and the redeemed are returning praise for their salvation.

11. By bearing much fruit

"In this is my Father *glorified*, that ye bear much fruit; so shall ye be my disciples" (John 15:8, italics added). When our lives produce righteous attitudes and actions, God is glorified.

B. Characterized

1. The refusal to glorify God

We have been looking at the positive side: what it means to glorify God. But the rejectors of this world are not interested in that, and so they live in violent and direct opposition to that which glorifies God. That is the characterization of all of the human race, apart from regeneration: "For all have sinned, and come short of the glory of God" (Rom. 3:23). Such men refuse to honor God and give Him thanks for all He has provided for them. When man fails to glorify the proper source of blessing, namely God, he replaces that source with himself, thinking that he is to be glorified. A perfect illustration of this is seen in the person of Nebuchadnezzar in Daniel 4:30-37:

Nebuchadnezzar was one of the greatest monarchs in the history of the world, and, while refusing to glorify God, he boasted in the glory of his own achievements: "The king spoke, and said, Is not this great Babylon, that I have built for the house of the kingdom by the might of my power, and for the honor of my majesty? While the word was in the king's mouth, there fell a voice from heaven, saying, O King Nebuchadnezzar, to thee it is spoken, The kingdom is departed from thee. And they shall drive thee from men, and thy dwelling shall be with the beasts of the field; they shall make thee to eat grass like oxen, and seven times shall pass over thee, until thou know that the Most High ruleth in the kingdom of men, and giveth it to whomsoever he will" (vv. 30-32). Because Nebuchadnezzar refused to glorify God, God took away his kingship and caused him to become a raving maniac.

But unlike most men, Nebuchadnezzar learned something from the chastening of the Lord: "And at the end of the days I, Nebuchadnezzar, lifted up mine eyes unto heaven, and mine understanding returned unto me, and I blessed the Most High, and I praised and honored him who liveth forever, whose dominion is an everlasting dominion, and his kingdom is from generation to generation. . . . Now I, Nebuchadnezzar, praise and extol and honor the King of heaven, all whose works are truth, and his ways justice; and those that walk in pride he is able to abase" (vv. 34, 37). It's my guess that you'll see Nebuchadnezzar in heaven, but he had to learn the hard way that God is to be glorified.

2. The results of not glorifying God

   a) Darkness

   Do you remember the results of rejecting God? Men "became vain in their imaginations, and their foolish heart was darkened" (Rom. 1:21*b*). They went from truth to emptiness, and then to darkness. Darkness in the Bible is seen in two ways:

   (1) Intellectual—"Gentiles walk, in the vanity of their mind, having the understanding darkened, being alienated from the life of God through the ignorance that is in them, because of the blindness of their heart" (Eph. 4:17*b*-18; cf. Ps. 119:105, 130).

   (2) Moral—This darkness has shown itself in the form of moral perversion throughout man's history (cf. Rom. 1:21-32).

   So man has forfeited understanding and virtue.

   b) Deception

   Paul cautioned us in Colossians 2 about the vanity of philosophy or human wisdom. "Beware lest any man spoil you through philosophy and vain deceit, after the tradition of men, after the rudiments of the world, and not after Christ" (v. 8). Philosophy is an empty illusion—it purports to be something, yet it is nothing but that which can ravage the soul. Human wisdom merely results in regression to the basic perversions of the human mind, devoid of God and lost in the blackness of sin.

III. RATIONALIZATION (v. 22)

"Professing themselves to be wise, they became fools."

The third reason God has a right to judge man is that man has rationalized that he can make right conclusions, even after having rejected the source of truth. When man refuses to accept truth, he destroys his power to discriminate. Of course man is going to pronounce himself wise in spite of the fact that he has rejected the God of wisdom. Hence, he is forced to rationalize; for who would willingly admit he was a fool and had made the worst mistake of all time?

It's very frustrating for me to hear people who have refused God's wisdom independently hypothesize about what they believe is right or wrong. And unfortunately, many Christians have been intimidated by the relative "truths" of impaired thinking and have compromised God's absolute truth.

A. Compromise

1. Theistic evolution

   Years ago many Christians decided they just had to believe in evolution because they were intimidated by those who "scientifically" believed that apparent discrepancies between the Bible and science could be best explained by the theory of evolution.

2. Liberal theology

   Many schools and churches have been ruined by the theology of liberals because people have been intimidated by their supposed intellectualism. In this regard, David Martyn Lloyd-Jones wrote: "The whole drift toward modernism that has blighted the church of God and nearly destroyed its living gospel may be traced to an hour when men began to turn from revelation to philosophy." In other words, when man stopped listening to God's Word, he decided he wanted to listen to the philosophy of men; and as a result, countless Christian institutions have compromised the absolute truth for half-truths and lies.

3. Psychology

   People think that psychologists have all the answers. The problem is that without the revelation of God they can only deal with symptoms of man's problems rather than the ultimate cause—man is not rightly related to his Creator. Men think they're wise in their own conceited, self-styled perception, but in reality they are "fools" (Rom. 1:22).

B. Confrontation

Now mark this carefully: Philosophy is set against the gospel when the "wisdom" of man is set above the wisdom of God. Paul makes this abundantly clear in 1 Corinthians 1: "For Christ sent me not to baptize but to preach the gospel; not with wisdom of words, lest the cross of Christ should be made of no effect. For the preaching of the cross is to them that perish foolishness; but unto us who are saved it is the power of God. For it is written, I will destroy the wisdom of the wise, and will bring to nothing the understanding of the prudent. Where is the wise? Where is the scribe? Where is the disputer of this age? Hath not God made foolish the wisdom of this world? For after that, in the wisdom of God, the world by wisdom knew not God, it pleased God by the foolishness of preaching to save them that believe. . . . Because the foolishness of God is wiser than men" (vv. 17-21, 25a).

The wisdom of this world is mere foolishness. Don't be intimidated by it, for what has worldly wisdom ever done to transform lives or to save man from his constant decline? It is utterly impotent. The blunt, clear message delivered by uneducated Christians with transformed lives infinitely exceeds the tangled, confused complications of human philosophy, because what man's wisdom *can't* do, God's foolishness *can*.

Now you see the decline and fall of man: revelation—God gave man the truth; rejection—man refused to believe it; rationalization—man affirms that the error he has invented is the truth, and he has convinced himself that he's right.

Focusing on the Facts

1. Who had more to say about judgment and hell than anyone else in Scripture (see pp. 62-63)?
2. Name several things that men will be judged for (see pp. 64-65).
3. What responsibility do believers have with God's revelation? Why (see p. 65)?
4. Support the fact that God responds to seeking hearts by citing verses in both the Old and New Testaments (see pp. 65-66).
5. Match the following verses to the practical ways in which Christians can glorify God (see pp. 66-68).

Philippians 2:11	Bearing fruit
1 Corinthians 10:31	Being morally pure
Joshua 7:19	Ministering one's gifts
Romans 4:20	Praising God
Psalm 50:23	Confessing sin
John 14:13	Confessing Jesus as Lord
1 Peter 4:10-11	Making God's glory our goal
2 Thessalonians 3:1	Trusting in God
1 Corinthians 6:18-20	Praying
2 Corinthians 4:15	Proclaiming the Word
John 15:8	Winning people to Christ

6. Whom did the monarch Nebuchadnezzar attempt to glorify through his boasting? What did he learn from the chastening of the Lord (Dan. 4:30-37; see pp. 68-69)?
7. Explain the nature of the darkness men enter when they refuse to glorify God (see p. 69).
8. When a man refuses to accept the truth, what does he destroy? Why is he forced to rationalize his refusal (see p. 70)?
9. How were many Christians intimidated to compromise their belief in a literal creation account (see p. 70)?
10. How have many Christian schools and churches been ruined (see p. 70)?
11. How can psychologists be limited when trying to deal with man's problems (see pp. 70-71)?
12. What has worldly wisdom ever done to transform lives or to save man from his constant decline (see p. 71)?

Pondering the Principles

1. Look over the many different reasons listed on pages 63-65 for the judgment of man. Choose the reasons for which you would be judged if you hadn't believed in Christ. Do you think you are subject to divine discipline for any of those things now that you are a Christian? Confess any sin you feel convicted of, asking God to supply you with the determination and wisdom you need to live a godly life.

2. In which of the ways of glorifying God listed on pages 66-68 are you weakest? Spend time in prayer this week, asking God to provide opportunities for you to glorify Him in those areas. Search Scripture for as much discussion on those topics as you can find.

3. Are you intimidated by humanistic philosophies that make Christianity and the Bible appear foolish? Do you find yourself wanting to compromise what you believe to be true because the majority of society doesn't believe in it? Don't give in to human wisdom that has divorced itself from God's wisdom. Although human wisdom can benefit man on a temporal basis, obeying divine wisdom can transform a man's life, grant him eternal life, guide him in pleasing his Creator, and result in heavenly rewards. Meditate on 1 Corinthians 1:18-2:8, memorizing 1:18 and 2:5. Be confident in the power of God's wisdom.

6
Reasons for the Wrath of God— Part 4

Outline

Introduction
A. The Proliferation of Religion
B. The Pursuit of Religion
C. The Paradox of Religion

Review
I. Revelation (vv. 19-20)
II. Rejection (v. 21)
  A. Its Reason Indicated
  B. Its Response Indicated
  C. Its Results Investigated
    1. Vain imaginations
    2. Darkened heart
III. Rationalization (v. 22)
IV. Religion (v. 23)
  A. The Descent into Idolatry
    1. Prohibited by God
    2. Performed by Israel
    3. Rejected by liberal theology
    4. Professed by ancient writings
      a) Extrabibilical
      b) Biblical
  B. The Deification in Idolatry
    1. The ultimate objects of worship
      a) Self
      b) Satan
    2. The immediate objects of worship
      a) "Creeping things"
      b) "Four-footed beasts"
      c) "Birds"
      d) "Corruptible man"

Introduction

A. The Proliferation of Religion

We live in a very religious world that is flooded with myriad religions and cults. At least 2.6 billion people in the world fall into one of these many identifiable religions. As far as the remaining 1.7 billion are concerned, it is interesting to note that demographers assume they have a religion, though it is unidentified with reference to any of the existing religious systems. Man is religious, and we don't have to look very hard to find examples to prove the point.

B. The Pursuit of Religion

Did you know that Hindus have some 330 million gods, which amount to about 8 per family? Besides all of these, the 450 million Hindus also worship 75 million cows.

For 400 million Buddhists, the most sacred object on earth is a two-inch-long discolored tooth believed to be the remnant of their founder, Buddha. Some even believe that statues of Buddha are actually living spirits.

Now the questions that must be asked are, Does all this religiosity of man prove that he is really seeking to know God? Is religion the progress of man struggling through his primitive confusion, the chaos of the world, and the traditions of his forefathers to reach the true God? Is man ascending through animism, polydemonism, and polytheism, arriving at monotheism and then finally worshiping the one *true* God? Should we pat men on the back and say, "We commend you for your pursuit of God?" Or, conversely, is man to be pitied because he's working so hard but just doesn't seem able to come up with the truth? Furthermore, if God sends that man to hell, as the Bible claims, isn't God being unfair to man who religiously is trying his best?

C. The Paradox of Religion

The answer to those questions is undoubtedly no. It is the

apostle Paul who gives this answer in Romans 1:19-23. He tells us that man does not *ascend* to religion; he *descends* to it.

Man is to be pitied—not because of a lack of opportunity, or because of his inability to see God clearly, or because God is unfair, but rather because he refuses the truth; and, having refused the truth at the highest level, he descends into the pit of religion. Man did not ascend out of the muck of paganism to discover God—he rejected the knowledge of God and descended into the muck of paganism.

Review

Man is thus held accountable by God because he should know better than to abandon the only absolute truth he has available to him. God, in His justice, demands that man face the consequence of his sin and rebellion. Romans 1:18 says, "The wrath of God is revealed from heaven against all ungodliness and unrighteousness of men, who hold the truth in unrighteousness."

That is the bad news Paul gives us before he presents the good news—first the danger, then the deliverer; first the judgment, then the way of escape; first the condemnation, then the forgiveness; first the guilt, then the grace. The whole message of forgiveness through the redeeming grace and love of God manifested for us by Christ on the cross, is based upon the presupposition that we under- stand that man is truly guilty of abandoning God's truth.

Furthermore, we must understand that God's perfect character demands that He react to sin in wrath. One writer, George Rogers, said, "[God's] righteous anger never rises, never abates: it is always at flood tide in the presence of sin because He is unchangeably and inflexibly righteous " (*Studies in Paul's Epistle to the Romans*, vol. 1 [Los Angeles: G. Rogers, 1936], p. 40). How could He who is infinitely holy disregard sin, which violates His utter holiness?

There are four reasons that God's anger is justified, being the appropriate response of a holy God to sin:

I. REVELATION (vv. 19-20; see pp. 34-40, 50, 65-66)

"Because that which may be known of God is manifest in them; for God hath shown it unto them. For the invisible things of him from the creation of the world are clearly seen, being understood by the things that are made, even His eternal power and Godhead, so that they are without excuse."

By observing creation, you can know of God's great power and supernatural character. A scientist said in this regard, "The phenomena of nature reveal the two qualities of force and intelligence working in perfect harmony." This is precisely Paul's message here.

Though this general revelation of God in creation is not enough to save man, it is instrumental in leading man to God's special revelation, the gospel of Christ, if man is honest in responding to the former. God wants men to know Christ (cf. 1 Tim. 2:4-7), so wherever He finds an eager, willing heart, He'll bring the message of Christ in some way to that person.

But men don't even live up to the light that they have. God is not under obligation to provide men more revelation.

II. REJECTION (v. 21; see pp. 50-59, 66-70)

"Because, when they knew God, they glorified him not as God, neither were thankful, but became vain in their imaginations, and their foolish heart was darkened."

A. Its Reason Indicated (John 3:19-21)

There's a very simple reason why men turn their backs on God: "For everyone that doeth evil hateth the light, neither cometh to the light, lest his deeds should be reproved" (v. 20; cf. v. 21). Men don't come to the light because they fear having their ungodliness and unrighteousness exposed. Men love their own darkness rather than God's light "because their deeds were evil" (v. 19); and for this rejection of revelation, man is condemned and stands guilty before his Creator.

B. Its Response Indicted (Daniel 5:23c)

Daniel's indictment of Belshazzar could be applied to everyone who has failed to honor and thank His Creator: "God, in whose hand thy breath is, and whose are all thy ways, hast thou not glorified." When man refuses to give glory to the One to whom it is due, he slides further away from God into empty darkness.

C. Its Results Investigated

1. Vain imaginations

Without God's truth, man is left with merely human philosophy. Now I want to make something very clear: I'm not totally against all human logic or reasoning. God has created man with a mind that has the capacity to reason, and every once in a while man has intersected with the truth. But when I talk about philosphy, I'm using the word in the more limited sense of "empty, useless reasoning, devoid of God," which is used by Paul in Colossians 2:8.

2. Darkened heart

When man's perception of truth becomes hopeless, clouded, confused, and uncertain, his heart is plunged into total darkness. It was to the Gentiles imprisoned in this intellectual and moral darkness that Paul was sent, "to open their eyes, and to turn them from darkness to light, and from the power of Satan unto God" (Acts 26:18a).

III. RATIONALIZATION (v. 22; see pp. 70-71)

"Professing themselves to be wise, they became fools."

Men who have seen the light of truth and then rejected it must affirm that their darkness is the truth. Like Pilate who asked Jesus, "What is truth?" (John 18:38a), a man who has not been born again by the Spirit of God is unable to ascertain what is true—what he *thinks* is true is merely the product of self-deception.

Paul informed Timothy that "evil men and seducers shall become worse and worse, deceiving, and being deceived" (2 Tim. 3:13). And to Titus he admitted, "For we ourselves also were once foolish, disobedient, deceived" (Titus 3:3a). Unregenerate man lives under the illusion, as did Lucifer and the nation Israel as well, that all wisdom and knowledge reside with him. God indicted Israel for their prideful deception: "Thy wisdom and thy knowledge, it hath perverted thee; and thou hast said in thine heart, I am, and none else beside me" (Isa. 47:10).

But do you know something? Even in the midst of his human philosophy and befuddled mind, and in the blackness of his heart, man still has a residual knowledge that God must exist.

IV. RELIGION (v. 23)

"And changed the glory of the incorruptible God into an image made like corruptible man, and birds, and four-footed beasts, and creeping things."

Man must have a God. Because there's a pulling of the supernatural dimension on his finite nature, religion becomes the fulfillment of his innate drive to worship. But as man has already rejected the true God, he must find a substitution for his reverence and therefore invents a god created according to his own speculation.

A. The Descent into Idolatry

Someone once said, "God made man in His own image and man returned the favor." The worst blasphemy against God is for man to fashion idols of the false gods whom he worships. This is made clear in the Ten Commandments, where idolatry is:

1. Prohibited by God

"And God spoke all these words, saying, I am the Lord thy God, who have brought thee out of the land of Egypt, out of the house of bondage. *Thou shalt have no other gods before me. Thou shalt not make unto thee any carved image, or any likeness of anything* that is in heaven above, or that is in the earth beneath, or that is in the water under the earth; thou shalt not bow down thyself to them, nor serve them; for I, the Lord thy God, am a jealous God, visiting the iniquity of the fathers upon the children unto the third and fourth generation of them that hate me" (Ex. 20:1-5, italics added). Rule number 1: No other gods. Rule number 2: No idols of any shape or form. That is the highest standard, and it is summed up in this statement of our Lord: "The first of all the commandments is: Hear, O Israel: The Lord our God is one Lord; and thou shalt love the Lord thy God with all thy heart, and with all thy soul, and with all thy mind, and with all thy strength: this is the first commandment" (Mark 12:29-30). In other words, if you are utterly committed to the true God, there is absolutely no place for any other god.

When men become religious apart from the true God, they have blasphemously violated God's standard. God demands first place in our lives. Have you given your Creator the place of priority in yours?

2. Performed by Israel

Unfortunately Israel hadn't given their Redeemer first place. Though God had sent prophets to Israel to turn them back from their evil ways, "Notwithstanding, they would not hear, but hardened their necks, like the neck of their fathers, who did not believe in the Lord their God. And they rejected his statutes, and his covenant that he made with their fathers, and his testimonies which he testified against them; and they followed vanity, and became vain, and went after the nations who were round about them, concerning whom the Lord had charged them, that they should not do like them. And they left all the commandments of the Lord their God, and made them melted images, even two calves, and made an idol, and worshiped all the host of heaven, and served Baal" (2 Kings 17:14-16). This is the decline of man that we've been tracing in Romans 1. Though God had revealed himself to Israel, He was rejected by them, and they consequently descended into vanity and idolatry.

This is the chronicle of how it is with men. Remember, man is not religious because he is ascending in his attempt to find God; he is religious because he is running away from God into the pit of idolatry.

3. Rejected by liberal theology

Despite the fact that the Bible, as well as history, supports the reality of man's devolution into idolatry, liberal theology deviates from the truth by claiming that man started in primitive forms of idolatry like animism and totemism, evolved up to polydemonism and polytheism, and finally arrived at monotheism. This is why it denies the Mosaic authorship of the Pentateuch. Liberalism believes that belief in one God developed at a much later time than that of Moses.

4. Professed by ancient writings

If the world was created in a perfect state, it is obvious to conclude that man is going downhill because of sin. These witnesses attest to man's descent into idolatry:

a) Extrabiblical

(1) Varro, a Roman scholar from the first century B.C., said that the Romans had no animal or human image of a god for 170 years after the founding of Rome (Augustine *The City of God* 4:31).

(2) Herodotus, the Greek historian from the fifth century B.C., said that the Persians had no temples or idols (*The Histories* 1:31).

(3) Lucian, the second century Greek prose writer, bears a similar testimony for Greece and Egypt concerning idols (*The Syrian Goddess* 34).

(4) Eusebius, the fourth century church historian, summed up the theory of antiquity when he said, "The oldest peoples had no idols."

(5) Horace, the Roman poet and satirist of the first century B.C., wrote, "I was a fig tree's trunk, a useless log. The workman wavered, 'Shall I make a stool or a god?' he chose to make a god, and thus a god I am."

(6) The Apocrypha says that an experienced woodcutter will cut down a tree that is easy to handle, strip off the bark, and with pleasing workmanship make a useful article that serves life's needs. But this woodcutter also will take a castoff piece (one that is good-for-nothing, a crooked stick full of knots), carve it with care, and cause it to resemble a man or a worthless animal while covering the blemishes with paint. He will then make a suitable niche for it, set it in the wall, and fasten it with iron—making sure that it does not fall because it cannot help itself. Then he will pray to it about possessions, his marriage, and his children—appealing for health from a thing that is weak, life from a thing that is dead, aid from an object that is thoroughly inexperienced, and strength from a thing whose hands have no strength (Wisdom of Solomon 13:11-19).

Those were some thoughts of the ancients. They all thought idolatry was really foolish, and yet they were trapped in the crowd of God rejectors with little in the way of alternatives.

b) Biblical

Isaiah 44 records God's indictment of the folly of idolatry: "Thus saith the Lord, the King of Israel, and his redeemer, the Lord of hosts: I am the first, and I am the last, and beside me there is no God. . . . Is there a God beside me? Yea, there is no God; I know not any. They that make a carved image are all of them vanity; and their delectable things shall not profit; and they are their own witnesses; they see not, nor know, that they may be ashamed. Who hath formed a god, or melted and cast an image that is profitable for nothing? Behold, all his fellows shall be ashamed; and the workmen, they are of men. Let

81

them all be gathered together, let them stand up; yet they shall fear, and they shall be ashamed together" (vv. 6, 8b-11).

So we see that man is religious, and when he rejects the true God he invariably makes a god of his own creation. This doesn't necessarily mean, however, that he always worships a literal idol. Man's idolatry can be internal as well as external.

B. The Deification in Idolatry

1. The ultimate objects of worship

    a) Self

    Because man invents deities like himself, he becomes, in effect, his own object of worship: "They worship the work of their own hands, that which their own fingers have made" (Isa. 2:8b). Man has always sought to acquire power and praise. When man worships his own creation, this fantasy (epitomized in ones such as Lucifer, Nebuchadnezzar, and the Antichrist) becomes realized. Now you probably are able to see how people can egotistically worship themselves, but you may wonder why would they worship inanimate objects such as sticks or stones. To understand that, we need to look at who is behind idolatry:

    b) Satan

    "But I say that the things which the Gentiles sacrifice, they sacrifice to demons, and not to God" (1 Cor. 10:20a). Why? Because if you want to worship an idol, a demon will impersonate the god you think resides there and will perform enough supernatural phenomena to retain your allegiance.

There's only one God. To worship anything else is to worship self and Satan.

2. The immediate objects of worship

    Let's look at the categories of idols that are worshiped by man, starting from the end of verse 23 and moving backward.

    a) "Creeping things"

    Do you know that people through the centuries have worshiped all sorts of crawling things like flies,

82

beetles, and snakes? In ancient Egypt, people worshiped scarab beetles.

b) "Four-footed beasts"

Remember the Israelites' golden calf at Mount Sinai (Ex. 32) and the pair of calf-idols set up at Bethel and Dan by Jeroboam (1 Kings 12)?

The Egyptians actually worshiped live bulls, and when one died they would bury it in a massive sarcophagus. The bull, however, was only one of the 20,000 different animals the Egyptians worshiped, not to mention the sun, moon, and stars.

c) "Birds"

The eagle, worshiped by the Romans, became a cause of religious conflict with the Jews, who recognized this Roman idol to be forbidden by divine law.

American Indians worshiped birds, having put them on their totems as thunderbirds.

d) "Corruptible man"

The gods of Greece and Rome were manlike in quality, as is evident from their mythology. Even emperor worship existed in the Roman Empire.

The Gods of America

You may think that only a few weird people somewhere worship most of these gods we've been talking about, yet here in America we have more "sophisticated" gods—but idols nevertheless. This nation's idolatry is generally "socially acceptable." We worship things like science, secularism, humanism, nationalism, naturalism, ecology, money, pleasure, sex, romance, entertainment, sports, education, prestige, power, rock singers, movie stars, great athletes—look at how many of these things hold the first place of concern in most peoples' lives. Make no mistake about it—America is idolatrous!

C. The Destiny of Idolatry

When religious man wipes God out of his life, all he's left with is himself. Consequently, he either substitutes himself directly or some other postulation of a god for the true object of worship. As if this were not blasphemous enough, the vast majority of mankind unknowingly worships the god of this world—Satan (cf. 2 Cor. 4:4; 11:14).

The man who continues in idolatry is destined for the final descent into reprobation. In the balance of Romans 1:24-32, Paul describes this state of reprobation in all its unrighteousness and wickedness. Because man has willfully rejected God in the face of God's clear revelation of Himself, God has revealed His wrath against the ungodliness of men by punishing them with their own sinfulness. This is why, three times, you read in this passage of reprobation: "Wherefore, God also gave them up" (v. 24*a*); "For this cause God gave them up" (v. 26*a*); and finally, "God gave them over to a reprobate mind" (v. 28*b*). Man without God, left to himself, becomes a prisoner of his own ungodliness. Neither man's philosophy nor his religion has the power to retard his vile sinfulness. There is only one thing that has that ability.

Conclusion

A. The Delight of God

God does not delight in punishment but rather in mercy: He is "not willing that any should perish, but that all should come to repentance" (2 Pet. 3:9*b*). "As I live, saith the Lord God, I have no pleasure in the death of the wicked, but that the wicked turn from his way and live; turn ye; turn from your evil ways; for why will ye die?" (Ezek. 33:11).

It is God's delight to show mercy and to shower upon man His grace, but this is no way alters the fact that He will allow the impenitent to suffer the consequences of their sins. God's attitude was perfectly expressed by our Lord: "O Jerusalem, Jerusalem, killing the prophets and stoning those who are sent to you! How often would I have gathered your children together as a hen gathers her brood under her wings, and you would not!" (Luke 13:34, RSV). "And when He drew near and saw the city He wept over it, saying, 'Would that even today you knew the things that make for peace! But now they are hid from your eyes. For the days shall come upon you, when your enemies will cast up a bank about you and surround you, and hem you in on every side, and dash you to the ground, you and your children within you, and they will not leave one stone upon another in you; because you did not know the time of your visitation'" (Luke 19:41-44, RSV). In the heart of God there are tears mingled with His wrath as He calls for men to respond to His grace.

B. The Decision of Man

You need not experience God's wrath. You can call on the Lord Jesus Christ and be delivered from it. If you don't worship the true God, then you are guilty, and you will spend eternity in hell paying for your guilt. That's your choice. Even though you may be very religious, that doesn't get you closer to God. Won't you open up your heart and life to the true God revealed through His Son, Jesus Christ?

Focusing on the Facts

1. Does the religiosity of man prove he is really seeking to know God? Is religion the progress of man struggling through the traditions of his forefathers to reach the true God? Is religion the evolution of polytheism to monotheism? Explain (see p. 75).
2. Why should man be pitied in his religious pursuits (see p. 76)?
3. Although the _____ revelation of God in creation is not sufficient to _____ man, it is instrumental in _____ man to God's _____ revelation, the gospel of Christ (see p. 77).
4. Why don't men readily come to the light of divine truth (John 3:19-21; see p. 77)?
5. In what sense does Paul use the term "philosophy" in Colossians 2:8 (see pp. 77-78)?
6. Why was Paul sent to the Gentiles, according to Acts 26:18 (see p. 78)?
7. Why must man worship some kind of a god? If he has already rejected the true God, what must he do (see p. 79)?
8. What is the worst blasphemy against God (see p. 79)?
9. Summarize the first two of the Ten Commandments. How did Jesus summarize the essence of them in Mark 12:29-30 (see p. 79)?
10. Why did God send prophets to speak to His people? How did they respond, according to 2 Kings 17:14-16 (see pp. 79-80)?
11. What is liberal theology's thesis regarding man's development of religion (see p. 80)?
12. What did some ancient writers says about idolatry (see pp. 80-81)?
13. What are the ultimate objects of worship in any form of idolatry (see p. 82)?
14. Give some example of idols that man has worshiped in ancient as well as in modern times (see pp. 82-83).
15. Whom does the vast majority of mankind unknowingly worship (see p. 83)?

16. What is the man who continues in idolatry destined for (see p. 83)?

17. What does God do to those who continually reject Him (Rom. 1:24, 26, 28; see p. 84)?

18. Does God delight in punishment? Support your answer with Scripture. Will He allow the impenitent to suffer the consequences of their sins (see p. 84)?

19. How can you avoid experiencing God's wrath (see pp. 84-85)?

Pondering the Principles

1. The supernatural dimension prompts a man to worship something greater than himself. Knowing that people have an innate need to worship, we should be prepared to direct them to the only worthy object of worship: God, our Creator. Memorize Romans 1:20 to show that the general revelation of creation should lead men to an awareness of God: "Since the creation of the world God's invisible qualities—his eternal power and divine nature—have been clearly seen, being understood from what has been made, so that men are without excuse (NIV). Memorize John 1:18 to show that the special revelation of Christ should lead men to a saving knowledge of Him: "No one has ever seen God, but God the One and Only, who is at the Father's side, has made him known" (NIV). When people understand that God has revealed Himself through His creation (Ps. 19:1; 139:13-14), and more specifically through His Son (Heb. 1:1-3), they need to act upon that knowledge by believing in Christ. In John 6:28, a crowd asks Jesus, "What must we do to do the works God requires?" (NIV). Memorize Jesus' answer: "The work of God is this: to believe in the one whom he has sent" (John 6:29, NIV). Pray for an opportunity to communicate these truths with someone this week.

2. What idols did you worship before committing your life to Christ? As a Christian, are there still possessions, goals, causes, hobbies, pleasures, or famous people that demand more devotion than you offer to Christ? Prayerfully mediate on Mark 12:28-34. Why do you love God? Apart from telling Him so, how does God know that you love Him? What do John 14:15 and 1 John 5:3 teach us? Do you think your love for Him is evident to others? What can you do to increase that love?

Scripture Index